From
BROKENNESS
to WHOLENESS
My Journey

GIGI LIONEL

WESTBOW
PRESS®
A DIVISION OF THOMAS NELSON
& ZONDERVAN

WestBow Press books may be ordered through booksellers or by contacting:

WestBow Press
A Division of Thomas Nelson & Zondervan
1663 Liberty Drive
Bloomington, IN 47403
www.westbowpress.com
1 (866) 928-1240

ISBN: 978-1-5127-8398-8 (sc)
ISBN: 978-1-5127-8400-8 (hc)
ISBN: 978-1-5127-8399-5 (e)

Library of Congress Control Number: 2017905943

Print information available on the last page.

WestBow Press rev. date: 5/11/2017

This book is dedicated to my son and daughter. You are my inspiration, my pride and joy. Thoughts of you kept me going even when I felt like giving up. I love you both unconditionally.

Here also is a special dedication to my best friend, Jen. Thank you for always being there and for your love, support, and encouragement through my darkest hours. I am thankful that our paths crossed some thirty-four years ago. You are a true friend.

This book is also dedicated to all those who share my unfortunate history of physical, emotional, and sexual abuse, the pain of infidelity, and the task of single parenting.

CONTENTS

FOREWORD

$\mathcal{I}$ have known the author for many years, but I never heard her story until she gave her testimony as a part of Celebrate Recovery, a Christ centered 12 - step program that help people overcome their hurts, habits and hang-ups. My reaction was "Wow! And to think she is still standing!" Some would not have survived what she has gone through. By the grace of God, though, today she is a loving mother, nurse, counselor, and, most importantly, a disciple of Jesus Christ. She truly is a living testimony to the grace of God that redeems, restores, and heals our hurts and emotions.

As I read *From Brokenness to Wholeness*, it made me think of two words used many times in the Bible: "But God ..." Again and again those two words are used as a turning point in bad situations, bringing forth hope and healing. Satan may think he has the upper hand in destroying people, but when God steps in, the situation will ultimately change.

I believe this short book is a valuable read for anyone who has been abandoned, physically abused, sexually molested, or betrayed. It offers sound advice to childcare workers and parents. It demonstrates hope even for those who feel that there is no way out.

—Pastor D. Shoemaker

Growing up, I felt that Mom was overprotective. I didn't understand her traumas until now. I'm thirty-four years old. Having been there through my parents' constant breakups, in my early twenties, I used to ask myself, "Why did she and my dad have me? What was the point?" It generated a lot of resentment, and it made me very cold toward my family. It wasn't until my early thirties that I realized my mom had suffered a terrible upbringing that was unfit for any child. My resentment quickly turned into more love and respect. Most importantly, I have a better understanding of what drives her and why she is the way she is. You can't fault someone on the results of past experience, only respect the fact that the person made it through that experience. In hindsight, looking at the big picture, I've realized that I am actually blessed because I was born to a mother who is one of the kindest, most loving and self-sacrificing people I know. I appreciate all that she has done for me. My mother worked her behind off to give my sister and me what we needed.

—S. G. Norbert

INTRODUCTION

What is wrong with me? And why me?

These are two questions I would constantly ask myself. For decades I felt like a failure and wondered why those painful things happened to me. Why couldn't I have been born into a loving family, nurtured by both father and mother? Why did I have to endure ongoing sexual abuse as an innocent child? Why did I have to have my heart broken through the constant infidelity of my spouse and by physical and emotional abuse? Why couldn't my marriage last till death do us part instead of ending in divorce? These and other questions would pop up now and then. One day I realized that all my pain was really an opportunity to let the world know that it does not matter what curveball life throws— by God's grace and mercy, you can rise above your circumstances and live a victorious life. It's one matter to write and give counsel to people when you have not experienced certain tribulations, but there is special power in the writings and counsel of the person who has experienced and survived those tribulations. So today I feel blessed to be able to share with the world my pain, my hurt, my disappointments, and my broken dreams. I hope that as you read my story, you will find hope and encouragement and that my pain will become someone else's healing balm.

From Brokenness to Wholeness is my story of how shattered I was because of the situations I encountered from childhood to middle adulthood—and how, only by God's grace and healing power, I was able to overcome those obstacles. I have now moved from feeling isolated, unloved, ashamed, guilty, sad, contemptuous of myself, and unforgiven to feeling connected, loved, forgiven, healed, guilt-free, unashamed, and free of blame.

So, as I take off my mask, I invite you into my world. Come now, settle down, perhaps with a cup of tea or coffee, and take a roller-coaster ride with me. Be careful … don't spill your drink.

PART 1

Abandoned but Not Forgotten

"Do not fear, for I have redeemed you; I have summoned you by name; you are mine. When you pass through the waters, I will be with you; and when you pass through the rivers, they will not sweep over you. When you walk through the fire, you will not be burned; the flames will not set you ablaze. For I am the Lord, your God, the Holy one of Israel, your Savior."

—Isaiah 43:1b, 2, 3b (NIV)

Even if my father and mother abandon me the LORD will hold me close.

—Psalm 27:10 (NLT)

The pitter-patter of the raindrops against the galvanized roofing resonated in twangs of unearthly melodies throughout the house. I always loved the rain. It helped me think. As I stared into my reflection, I slowly began to fade as the world outside came into focus. Trees were slowly swinging back and forth in the moderate storm. They reminded me of how Gramma would sway back and forth in the pew on Sundays. As I continued to stare at the trees, they reminded me of myself—moving in one direction but getting thrown in the other, all the while staying in the same place. My thoughts wandered to my childhood days, and I thought how every child brought into this world deserves proper care, love, and nurturing as part of an excellent upbringing—this is the key to a good quality of life for children.

The creak in the floorboard behind me caused me to flinch, but I did not turn around; I heard his voice call me, but I did not listen. I knew that, minutes later, I would find myself embraced by his dirty hands. It was still raining when he was done. His exit was preceded by the familiar sound of our dilapidated wooden door hitting the doorstop.

It was still raining when I went back to the window. As before, I saw my reflection first—although it was different this time. I let my thoughts wander again. I often wondered why such crimes were committed against children. Molested, beaten, abused, and abandoned—to such treatment I am no stranger. I came into this world with a bag of bricks on my back—how was I still alive? The rain had stopped. To my dismay, the trees were still; now it was time to go to the banana plantation.

I am the second of four siblings and hardly knew my dad while growing up. I have vague memories of him holding me and giving me cookies and milk but not much else. I also have flashbacks of him and my mom arguing and fighting. According to my mom, my dad was an alcoholic who often fought with her after he had been drinking. My mom left my dad when I was around four and my youngest sister was just one year old. After the separation, my father migrated to Barbados, where he died several years later from a combination of alcohol and medication.

I am not sure why, but my mom took my sister and me to live with my grandmother and auntie. Both lived in another town about twenty-four hours away. I was practically raised by my grandmother, auntie, and other nearby relatives. We lived in the country, and I had to walk back and forth about two hours to school, which was located in the city.

My mom soon had another child, whom she also placed in my grandmother's care. I do not know what happened, but shortly after this, my mom came back and took my brother and sister, leaving me alone. I was devastated and could not understand why I was the one left behind.

That was the first time I genuinely felt abandoned. I was in shock because my abandonment was completely unexpected. I was confused because I did not know what it all meant. Was I a bad girl? Did someone tell my mom that I had done something wrong? These thoughts awakened feelings of guilt and shame in me. What made my situation even worse was that no one had any answers for me, so my imagination ran wild. I experienced fear and grief about my separation from my brother and sister, thinking that, perhaps, they went with my mom because they were better than I was—or could it be that my mother loved them more than she loved me? These and other feelings caused me to have low self-esteem while growing up. Have you ever felt abandoned as a child? I believe it's the most grievous loss a child can suffer. I felt unlovable and unimportant despite how genuinely nurturing my auntie and grandma were.

A child is conceived from a sexual encounter. Once the child is born, some mothers, as well as some fathers, walk away as if they were returning an item to the store. That's the saddest event because the baby never has a chance to bond with his or her family, and this creates a void that, in some instances, can never be filled. I understand there can be reasons a parent feels he or she needs to abandon a child. Some mothers abandon their children by putting them in the care of relatives because they can't cope with all the stress and responsibility that comes with a newborn. Some have no inbred mothering skills, want their freedom, are not financially able to care for the baby, or perhaps just can't deal with having to provide for a child. On the other hand, some mothers are drug addicts or alcoholics, and they love their children enough to give them away to relatives rather than raise them in an environment that is not in the best interest of the child.

My mom, however, never gave me a good reason why she left me. I can only assume that it was hard for her as a single parent, lacking education and unable to find work in order to care for the three of us. Perhaps she thought it would be much easier to care for two children than three, and since I was the oldest, she left me, thinking I would be best able to cope. She probably never considered that my grandma and aunt were not working either and had to struggle to care for me. As a child, I was unable to comprehend or process all of this. All I knew was that I had been left behind.

Still, I had my auntie. I was very fond of her because she took good care of me and instilled godly values in me, including the habit of churchgoing. She taught me always to respect people who were older than me. She always protected me, and I began to feel as though she were actually my mom. Yet I can still recall feeling very sad as I longed for the love that only a mom and dad can provide.

Growing up, we regularly attended an evangelical church in the city. I loved attending the prayer meetings and open-air services. It was during one of these meetings that I had my first encounter with my higher power, Jesus Christ. At this very young age, reading the Bible and learning about God brought joy, peace, and comfort to my soul. I accepted the Lord as my personal Savior, and I was baptized at the age of seven.

Perhaps you felt abandoned as a child, and even now, years later, you find yourself still carrying the pain or effects of abandonment. Your mood may still be a mixture of various and contradictory emotions such as guilt, shame, anxiety, fear, or frustration. You may be in denial of the abandonment, or you may choose the role of victim. Whatever it may be, these emotions continue to cause the unhealed wounds to fester, and they may promote addictions, self-neglect, and relationship issues. In Psalm 27:10 (NLT), we read, "Even if my father and mother abandon me, the LORD will hold me close." So even if you have been forsaken or abandoned by your dearest relatives, whether your parents or others, take comfort in the knowledge that the one relative who will never abandon you is God, your eternal Father. God's love is stronger and more certain than even the closest human relative's. The Lord will gather you up into his arms and bosom, and he will shield you under his wings of protection. The Lord will never forget or neglect you.

I slept on the floor in my grandma's room and often had visions of my mom standing at the bedroom door, wearing a black-and-white striped jumpsuit with a black hat. For some reason, she looked very real as she stood in the doorway, staring at me. I would jump up from my bedding on the floor and crawl into my grandma's bed, screaming so loudly that I would wake up everyone in the house. After I screamed, the image of my mom would just disappear. I did not know what these visions meant, but I had them quite often as a child—and they made me very fearful. My life became filled with fears of every kind—dark rooms, shadows, and loud noises would all make me afraid. My worst fear was barking dogs. The visions slowly disappeared as I got older, but the fears remained. I would jump and scream at shadows, especially in the night, when they were prevalent, and so I was given the nickname *Scaredy-cat*.

In the absence of my mom and dad, Jesus Christ became very real to me. In his Word, he promises never to leave us or forsake us, and I clung to this promise. Jesus became my mother, father, and friend. As a little girl, I knew to go to him for everything. I always prayed for God's protection over me. When I was eight, I memorized Psalm 91 and Psalm 23, and I would say them every morning and night and sometimes when I was walking alone.

I also learned in Sunday school that Jesus was Jehovah-Nissi, "Our Banner"—a banner of love and protection. As I made the two-hour journey alone to school every day, I prayed that God would protect me from dogs, tigers, wolves, and snakes. The trip to school each day was over the hills and through woods, valleys, and meadows, just like Little Red Riding Hood's journey, and by the time I got to school, I was often exhausted. I often ate half of my lunch before I got to school on days when I got very hungry and thirsty during the walk. Psalm 23 became my favorite as I prayed, "Yea though I walk through the valley of the shadow of death I will fear no evil for thou art with me thy rod and thy staff they comfort me." I always felt the presence of a second person walking and guiding me each step of my way, but I didn't know who or what it was. I now know that this was my guardian angel. I never prayed for God to keep me safe from bad people at that age. I guess I was not aware that bad people even existed until one day I heard about someone who was murdered in a house near the forest path I took to school. After I learned of this death, I added bad people to my list of dangers against which I asked God's protection. I ran like lightning each time I passed that house. I asked my auntie why I had to walk to school when other children took the van.

"Your mother is not sending money for you, and we have no money to give you," was her reply.

Walking to school, I encountered barking dogs and almost got bitten by one. I never encountered wolves, tigers, or snakes because they did not exist in that forest, only in the storybooks I read. God protected me and kept me from harm, and I am ever so thankful because anything could have happened to me on my way to school. Through it all, however, he kept me safe.

Reflection

Abandonment affects anyone who has been left behind, whether by divorce, adoption, separation, rejection, or fostering. At times in my life, even as an adult, my abandonment issues would sometimes resurface, and I would become overwhelmed with feelings of inadequacy. I felt unloved and suffered low self-esteem. All of these monsters would visit me now and again. Being a loner and staying away from my family are results of my abandonment as a child. I now know that I am a child of God. I am significant, and I am secure in him. More than that, I am accepted by him, and I believe his words when he gives me that blessed assurance that he will never leave me or forsake me. Blind songwriter Fanny Crosby penned the words to that beloved hymn "Blessed Assurance."

> Blessed assurance, Jesus is mine!
> O what a foretaste of glory divine!
> Heir of salvation, purchase of God,
> Born of his Spirit, washed in his blood.
>
> Perfect submission, perfect delight,
> Visions of rapture now burst on my sight;
> Angels descending bring from above
> Echoes of mercy, whispers of love.
>
> Perfect submission, all is at rest;
> I in my Savior am happy and blest,

Watching and waiting, looking above,
Filled with his goodness, lost in his love.

I have learned that you never have to walk through life alone. Your family doesn't have to be blood relatives. Jesus and your church family can serve as your family.

INNOCENCE LOST

Childhood should be carefree, playing in the sun; not living a nightmare in the darkness of the soul.

—Dave Pelzer, *A Child Called "It"*

Abuse manipulates and twists a child's natural sense of trust and love. Her innocent feelings are belittled or mocked and she learns to ignore her feelings. She can't afford to feel the full range of feelings in her body while she's being abused— pain, outrage, hate, vengeance, confusion and arousal. So she short-circuits them and goes numb. For many children, any expression of feelings, even a single tear, is cause for more severe abuse. Again, the only recourse is to shut down. Feelings go underground.

—Laura Davis, *Allies in Healing: When the Person You Love Is a Survivor of Child Sexual Abuse*

*M*y aunt soon left with her boyfriend for St. Croix, where they later got married. After she left, everything changed. Once again I felt that I was abandoned. This time it was by my aunt, the person who had really been taking care of me. I was taken out of school twice a week to work on the banana plantation. Bananas were the main export in St. Lucia at this time, and most people were farmers and depended on them for their livelihood. I remember dreading being taken out of school and would often cry, especially after I tripped and fell backward with a tray of bananas on my head and almost broke my neck.

Now that my auntie was gone, my uncle, who lived a couple of houses away, took on the task of disciplining me. Only rather than doing it with a spirit of love, he did it by beating the daylights out of me. I got many beatings. I cried because I did not want to be taken out of school. During those times, I felt like an eagle in a chicken coop; I did not belong here. I know that there was much more within me than I was experiencing. I remember telling myself that I had dreams and aspirations to become something more than just this person who was walking barefooted in mud while carrying bananas on her head. I wanted to do well in school and become someone; I just did not know what. What I did know was that I could not stay here in this type of life. I thought there had to be more to life than this hard work and drudgery. I would often daydream about my mom, brother, and sister, wondering if I would ever see them again. My mom would visit on rare occasions, and when she left, I always wished she would take me back with her.

Initially I was not doing well in school because of all the absences and tardiness, but I remember studying very hard, and my grades started to improve. One day I achieved 100 percent on a science test, and the teacher called me into the office to question whether I had cheated on the exam. I explained to her that I did not cheat but had studied very hard—that I really wanted to succeed in school despite being taken out of school regularly. From then on, I began to excel in school and became the teacher's pet.

I was around eight years old when the nightmare began. My grandma would send me to deliver food and run errands for an older male relative who was homebound and lived about thirty minutes away. He must have been about sixty years old, and on many occasions, he would sexually abuse me. He told me never to tell anyone because he would hurt me if I did. After a while, I would cry every time I was sent to visit him. Not knowing the reason for my tears, my relatives thought my reluctance was due to laziness and beat me for crying. This continued for many years until he finally died.

My grandmother sent me to live with another aunt. This aunt lived in the city, which was closer to my school. The journey was shorter, which was a blessing. However, just like the relative, my aunt's boyfriend started sexually abusing me. He would tell me to sit in his lap and then pretend to read to me. Sometimes my aunt was in the bedroom while we were in the living room; the abuse happened almost under her very nose. He warned me not to tell my aunt. If she found out, he said, she would not defend me. She would say that I was a bad girl, and I would get a beating from her. I didn't think anybody would deliver me from this horrible cycle of abuse, and I was all alone in my grief and agony. This continued for about two years. They finally broke up, and I went back to live with my grandmother in the country.

By then I felt very confused and angry. Where was God? I could not understand why he was allowing these bad things to happen to me. Better yet, where was my mom when all of this was happening? Why was I left behind where these horrible things could happen to me?

Because I was experiencing all these emotions, I started rebelling against everyone and everything. I stole money or anything I could find and got into a lot of trouble. I recall a time when I went into a shop and stole a huge piece of cheese when the storekeeper was busy. I did not really know why I took the cheese. I was not hungry; I just felt like acting out because I was angry.

I also started physically abusing younger children in the neighborhood. I would beat or pinch them for no reason until I made them cry. I hated myself and pretended to be two different people. On some occasions I would pretend to be happy, with no conscious knowledge of the abuse. I would be laughing and playing with the children in the yard. The next minute, I would have flashbacks of the sexual abuse and go numb. That's when I would physically abuse the other children. Whenever an abusive situation occurred, I would endure it or space out until it was over and then block it from my mind. I carried this secret with me, fearing that if I told my secret, anyone I told would not believe me or would think it was my fault. I was also being threatened.

In the summer of 1972, when I was about twelve years old, it happened again. This time I was visiting my eldest sister, who lived about an hour and a half away by bus in another town. I was introduced to this man who she said was a family friend. He started sexually abusing me. He often slept over and would slip into my room when everyone was asleep. He would cover my mouth to stop me from screaming. He told me this was our secret, and if I told my sister, he would kill me.

This treatment had become almost routine for me by that point, causing me to become even more confused. Not knowing what else to do, I started calling on the God I had prayed to in my younger years to protect me from bad people. Where was God, whom I trusted to be my mother, my father, and my friend? Was he blind? Was that why he could not see what was happening to me? Why wasn't he answering my prayer to stop the abuse? I had learned in Sunday school that God knows, hears, and sees all events. He is omnipresent—surely he must know, see, and hear what was happening to me and be present when I was suffering harm. But how could he be there, seemingly as a spectator, and not step in and stop it? I felt myself losing faith in the God I had imagined as loving and trustworthy. I started wondering: if God was not going to protect me, who would, and where could I turn? I was carrying around this secret and began to suppress it. It went on to create a hole in my soul during my tender years. I began to feel an overwhelming sense of shame and hopelessness. I thought that perhaps I was a bad child and deserved what was happening to me. This debilitating shame perpetuated the secret and kept me silent until the age of thirty-two.

I was in college, completing my Bachelor's in Nursing, when I took a psychology course. As part of the curriculum, I had to write an autobiography, explaining how events that happened to me as a child had affected me as an adult. It was very painful to recall the sexual abuse, and I cried hysterically as I poured everything out and placed it on paper. It was only then that I opened up and let the secret I had been holding for all those years come out.

I know now that the effects of sexual abuse extend far beyond childhood. Sexual abuse robs children of their childhood, creates a loss of trust, brings about feelings of guilt, and leads to self-abusive behavior. It can also lead to antisocial behavior, depression, identity confusion, loss of self-esteem, and other serious emotional problems. It can also lead to difficulty with intimate relationships later in life.

The sexual victimization of children is ethically and morally wrong. I believe the perpetrators should be severely punished. I was around fifteen when I heard that my aunt's ex- boyfriend was killed by a woman who pierced his heart with an ice pick. I do not know the details, but deep down in my heart, I thought he deserved it for what he had done to me and maybe to other children. I remember asking God why it took him so long to punish that man after what he had done to me.

If you are reading this book and have come across this page and have been sexually abused or molested, or if it is happening to you now, please tell someone. Often the perpetrator will threaten you, just as several such men threatened me, but you must not listen to them. The reality is that they are scared because they know what will happen to them if they are found out. What they are doing is so vile and wicked that even murderers and other criminals despise child molesters and often impose their own brand of justice on inmates who have harmed children.

You have options:

- **Contact someone you trust.** Many people feel fear, guilt, anger, shame, and/or shock after they have been sexually assaulted. Having someone there to support you as you deal with these emotions can make a big difference. It may be helpful to speak with a counselor, someone at a sexual assault hotline, or a support group.
- **Report what happened to the police.** If you do decide to report what happened, you will have a stronger case if you do not alter or destroy any evidence. This means that you should not shower, wash your hair or body, comb your

hair, or change your clothes, even if it is hard to refrain from doing those things. If you are nervous about going to the police station, it may help to bring a friend with you. There may also be sexual assault advocates in your area to assist you and answer your questions.

- **Go to an emergency room or health clinic.** It is very important for you to seek health care as soon as you can after being assaulted. You will be treated for any injuries and offered medications to help prevent pregnancy and STDs.

Parents, God has entrusted you with the lives of your children, who care about you, love you, and trust you. Most children who are sexually abused do not tell anyone about it and many keep their secret all their lives. A few children who have been abused may start talking to you about it. They may do so because they trust you and want to share the burdens they are carrying with you. Hearing a child talking about being abused is very difficult. You may react in different ways. Your reaction is very important to the child. If you react with disgust or don't believe your child, the child may stop talking to you about it. If the child trust you enough to tell you about the abuse you must remember that they rarely lie about such things. Although it may be hard to believe that someone we trust or care about is capable of sexually abusing a child, it's highly unlikely that a child would deliberately make false accusations about adult-like behaviors. If you do not believe the child he or she will feel that you don't trust him or her, and this will prevent that child from getting help. It also prevents the abuse from stopping. Be very sensitive and listen carefully when a child is talking to you about abuse. Keep in mind that it is very difficult for the child to talk about being abused. This is especially hard for children who have been sexually abused. The child has gathered up all of his or her courage to tell you about the abuse. How you handle the conversation will determine how you will be able to help your child.

In an article entitled "Talking to a Child who has been Abuse" authors Saraswathy Ramamoorthy and Judith A. Myers –Walls, Ph.D., share considerations to keep in mind when a child discloses abuse. These considerations includes:

- **Help the child feel comfortable.** Talking about abuse is not easy for the child. Respect the child's privacy and talk to him or her in a quiet and private place. The place should be familiar to the child. This will help the child feel comfortable.

- **Reassure the child that it is not his or her fault.** Most children who are abused feel that they are to blame for their own abuse. Their abusers very often tell them this is true. It is very important to reassure the child that she or he is not guilty and not responsible for the abuse. Let abused children know that they have not done anything wrong.

- **Don't react with shock, anger, or disgust.** Your reaction to what the child tells you is very important to the child, who will be watching your reaction very closely. Be calm. When you react with disgust or anger, even if it is at the perpetrator, the child will not feel comfortable talking to you anymore and may also feel scared and confused. This will prevent you from acting promptly and getting help immediately.

- **Don't force a child to talk.** Give the child time to talk to you at his or her own pace. If the child is unwilling to talk or seems uncomfortable, don't pressure the child to do so. If the child seems uncomfortable when talking about certain events, don't press for details. You can change the topic to an easier one at that point.

- **Don't force a child to show injuries.** If the child is willing to show you his or her injuries, allow the child to do so. However, when a child is unwilling to show injuries, do not insist. Do not insist that a child undress so that you can see the injuries.

- **Use terms and language that the child can understand.** If the child says something that you don't understand, like a word for a body part, ask the child to explain or point to it. Don't correct or make fun of the words the child uses. When you use the same words, the child may feel less confused and more relaxed. The child will feel that you understand him or her.

- **Don't "interview" the child.** The purpose of your discussion is to gather enough information to make an informed report to the local Child Protective Services agency or to the Police. When you have the information you need, stop the discussion. Don't try to prove that abuse has happened.

- **Ask appropriate questions.** The questions you ask the child must be appropriately worded. Choose your language carefully. This ensures that you get correct information from the child. For example, if you see a bruise on a child and suspect it is the result of abuse, you may ask the child, "That looks painful. Do you want to tell me how you got it?" or "Do you want to talk about that bruise you have?" It would be inappropriate to say, "Did you get that bruise when someone hit you?" Remember that you can do more harm by supplying a child with words and ideas. Let the child tell his or her own story and give you the answers.

- **Don't ask *why* questions.** These are questions like, "Why did he hit you?" or "Why did she do that?" They will only confuse a child more. Remember, children who are abused often do not understand why it is happening. Such questions will force them to think about the reasons for the abuse. *Why* questions also will not give you any helpful information.

- **Don't teach the child new terms or words.** Don't teach the child new words or give her or him new ideas. This is harmful. When you do this, you are influencing the child. Also, when you teach a child a new term or word, you are changing the child's original disclosure. This is important in relation to the court and the law.

- **Find out what the child wants from you.** A child may ask you to promise not to tell anyone. She or he may ask to be taken home with you or ask you what you are going to do. It is good to know what the child is expecting from you. This will help decide your course of action.

- **Be honest with the child.** Let the child know what you are going to do. Truthfulness will build trust. Be honest about what you can do and make no promises that you cannot keep. For example, tell the child that you may have to tell someone so that the child will not be hurt anymore. Then the child will not be surprised or afraid when he or she finds out that someone else knows.

- **Confirm the child's feelings.** Let the child know that it is okay to feel scared, hurt, confused, or angry.

- **Be supportive.** Let the child know that you are glad he or she told you about the abuse, that you believe what you were told, and that you care about the child. Some children may think that you will not like them anymore because of what they told you. Reassure them that you are still their friend.

- **Remember that the child's safety is the most important issue.** Be sensitive to and aware of the child's safety. Keep in mind that a child might be further abused if it becomes known that the child has spoken to you about the abuse. If you feel that the child is in danger, you must contact Child Protective Services (CPS) immediately.

For pastors, the first and most important step is to believe the survivor's story. Adults rarely fabricate this experience. Because of the shame involved, victims do not subject themselves to the potential rejection and scrutiny that sexual abuse survivors experience without a legitimate reason.

Next, honor the person's pain and the coping methods he or she may be using to survive. Historically, the church has often been guilty of shooting its wounded. In their zeal to respond aggressively to sin, church members have failed to offer grace and compassion to wounded people. The wise pastor will put first things first by clearly responding to the tragedy of sexual abuse before addressing any resulting issues.

The other point to remember is that victims have experienced spiritual wounds, and those who are helping them must accept their ambivalence or anger toward God. Provide a supportive environment for spiritual processing of the survivor's experience. Avoid putting a religious bandage on a gaping wound. Allow the victim to grieve and model ways of relating to the heavenly Father that may be unlike the helpers' ways.

Be supportive of the way the victim may be working through

recovery. Do not criticize the time and money spent on therapy or self-help groups. Do not rush the victim through the healing process or encourage the victim to forgive before he or she is ready. Recognize that the victim's family relationships are often complicated, especially if the family did not protect the victim or does not believe the abuse occurred. Many victims are estranged from family, at least for a time. Respect the boundaries they need to erect to feel safe.

Finally, be sure to refer the survivor for outside professional help. Assemble a list of Christian counselors in your area who are specifically equipped to treat sexual abuse victims. Know about helpful books, support groups, and other resources to which you can refer the victim.

Reflection

I prayed every night that God would take me away from that situation, but it did not happen. I always wondered why God did not answer my prayers and protect me and why he let the abuse continue. Everywhere I went, I found myself in a sexually abusive situation. The sexual abuse distorted my image of God and affected my ability to seek and trust him.

I know the truth now: God intimately understands the pain victims endure through their abuse. Victims do not choose abuse, but Jesus chose to subject himself to abuse, and because of that, we can trust in him; we can trust that he knows and empathizes with all the pain and humiliation that victim's experience. As for our eternal souls, no one can harm them.

The Lord does not cause abuse. The best of people can suffer evil treatment. Even if the abuse doesn't stop, it doesn't mean that God isn't watching over victims and giving them the strength to endure. God also gives us free will, and just as God will not violate my free will, he also will not violate the perpetrator's free will. God is not to be blamed for the abuse. The perpetrator, not God, made the choice to violate another human being. We can argue that God could have stopped it; yes, he could—because he is God. But sometimes he allows negative events to happen to us so that he can turn them around for his good. Now, as I have counseled clients, I clearly see how God is using my experiences to help bring healing to those who have also been sexually abused. I can identify with them and feel their pain because I have been there. Clients are comforted to know that it happened to me as well, and if God can heal me, he will heal them also.

Sexually abused children and teens often feel dirty and

ashamed because this is the root Satan intends for sexual abuse. He loves it when we loathe ourselves. One of the reasons he uses sexual abuse so effectively is because it destroys a woman's beauty—the part of God's image she portrays. Remember, Satan was a beautiful angel before he fell. I think that is one of the reasons he chose Eve instead of Adam; he hates a woman's beauty. So when he robs her of her childhood, her femininity, and her sexuality and replaces them with shame, guilt, and fear through sexual abuse, he wins, or so he thinks. Although childhood sexual abuse is a debilitating experience with potentially lifelong effects, it is not a death sentence. As our great physician, God offers healing and hope to the abused. There will always be scars, but individuals can move from victimhood to survivorship. God can transform violations that a perpetrator intended for harm into something good and amazing. The experience of sexual abuse can become only one thread in the tapestry of that survivor's history. The survivor can ultimately see how those threads have blended into the overall tapestry to create something that, from this side, looks like a tangled mess but is a beautiful work of art from God's side.

Jeremiah 29:11 (AMP) states, "For I know the thoughts *and* plans that I have for you, says the Lord, thoughts *and* plans for welfare *and* peace and not for evil, to give you hope in your final outcome." This verse tells us that God knows us and has good plans for us; he is the sovereign director of our lives. His words remind us that God hears our prayers and invites us to seek and know him. During times of uncertainty, this promise is deeply comforting. We cannot see the future, but this verse gives us encouragement and promises that God has a future and hope for each one of us, regardless of the situation or circumstances we might face.

God's plan isn't always what we thought it was going to be, but God's plan is always best, even if we don't understand it at the time. "And we that in all things God works for the good of those who love him, who have been called according to his purpose." Romans 8:28 (NIV). We know that God is working through every event in our lives to make us more and more dependent on him for everything we need. We need to realize that, although God's plan is not always the easiest in our eyes, it is always the best.

God sees our tomorrows before they become our todays. He not only sees the beginnings and ends of our lives; he also sees everything in between. In Psalm 139:16, (NIV) we read, "All the days ordained for me were written in your book before one of them came to be." God knows the plans he has for us.

REUNITED WITH MY MOM

Do not be afraid, for even now I hear the yearnings of your heart, and I am sending you my answer to your prayers. Though you may not know the ways of your journey, I am guiding you with my gentle touch. You are not alone. I hold you in my hands to protect you. Someday my plan for you will become clear and you will find peace. Until such time walk in faith. Remember—I love you. You are my child.

—Anonymous author

After visiting with my sister, I decided that I had had enough maltreatment. If God was not going to help me and make the bad people go away, I would go away from them. That summer, when I was twelve years old, I formulated a plan to get back to my mom. I told my grandmother that my mom had sent me a message at my sister's place, asking me to come live with her. I told my grandmother that my brother-in-law would take me to my mom's house. There had, in fact, been no message. In reality, I did not know where my mom lived or how to get there. However, I packed my few belongings and left for my mom's house with my sister's husband.

The journey to my mom's home took two days. I remember getting sick from all the travel; upon arrival to the city my sister's husband took me to the bus stop and left me there. Later in the day he returned to check on me, only to find that I was still waiting for a bus. He then took me to his sister's home where we spend the night. The next morning, he took me back to the bus stop and asked the bus driver to drop me in the town where my mother lived. I remembered feeling happy and anxious at the same time, as I did not know what to expect. I arrived at my mom's home late in the evening, only to find she was not home. The bus driver left me with a neighbor. I learned later that she was my father's sister.

My mom finally came home about an hour later and was very surprised to find me waiting for her. To my despair, rather than being overjoyed to see me, she was very upset and demanded to know what I was doing there and told me to go back where I came from. I remembered crying and telling her that I could not stay with my grandmother anymore. I also remember my sister crying and holding onto me. Since my mom had no other choice, she let me stay.

I turned thirteen that year. I never told my mom about the sexual abuse that I suffered through the years, partly because I did not know how; I was also afraid that she would reject me even more. From then on, I began to repress the reality of my sexual abuse.

I was very happy to be reunited with my sister and brother. My mom enrolled me in the primary school, where I did very well. I joined different clubs in the community; one of my favorite activities was the cricket team. We went to different parts of the country, competing with other teams.

Despite being reunited with my mom, I did not feel close to

her. She had missed my whole childhood. I could not relate to her because I did not really know her. What was even sadder, she did not express any love for me; maybe she did not know how to show love.

She was very strict, particularly when it came to boys. If she saw me walking or playing with a boy, she would get hysterical, and sometimes I would get a beating. I thought the beatings should have stopped, but I was wrong. My mom would beat my sister and me when our behavior was not in accordance with her rules, and very minor lapses could trigger her anger.

In spite of my mom's strictness, I became promiscuous and had many boyfriends. I was looking for the genuine love that I had never had, and I was looking for it in all the wrong places. I needed attention and longed to feel loved. Having been sexually abused did not help the situation either; teenage promiscuity is also a side effect of being sexually abused. At fifteen, I graduated from primary school and was accepted to secondary school. My mom told me that she was not able to send me because she did not have the money to pay for school or transportation to and from school. She also said that she would not waste her time and money on me because I was up to no good and would soon get pregnant.

I was very disappointed and upset. I went to the principal of my primary school and explained the situation to her. Since I was an excellent student, she offered me a job as a training teacher, teaching first-graders. This was a great opportunity for me. I was earning my own money while receiving an education.

At the age of sixteen, just as my mom had predicted, I got pregnant. I wondered what I was going to do. How was I going to tell my mom that I was pregnant? I remember thinking that she would kill me for sure.

When I went to live with my mom, I felt that my relationship with God was not what it should be. On Sundays I went to a Catholic church, as that was my mom's religion, and I felt it was not the same. After three years, I received a New Testament that also contained the Psalms from the Gideons when they visited my school. I read my New Testament at times, along with the Psalms, but there were no Bible studies or prayer meetings to attend. The Catholic and Seventh-day Adventist churches were the only ones in my town at that time. I did explore the Seventh-day Adventist Church, but their doctrine did not make sense to me. I can thank God for the seed that was planted in me in my early years.

During my years of abuse, I blamed God for it because, when I was a helpless child, he never helped me or caused the abuse to stop. But at that point, I felt it necessary to call upon him. I started really praying for God to help me; I did not know what to do. I remember asking him to take away the pregnancy, though I also told him that if it was his will, then let me keep it, but please make a way for me. I did not know how I would be able to care for this baby.

My boyfriend, who was actually the stepson of my mom's boyfriend, was making plans to build a small house for us to live in. Deep down inside, I knew this was not the life I wanted, and there had to be more. I did not want to be like other sixteen-year-olds who already had one or two babies, no education, and no idea where their next meal would come from. No, not me! I did not want that kind of life. I felt trapped, not knowing what to do. I started feeling sick from the pregnancy, which went unrecognized by my mom. In the second month, I finally got the courage to tell her that I was pregnant. To my surprise, she did not kill me. She just said, "I was expecting this to happen." I continued to pray for God's will. Luckily for me, in the third month, I had a miscarriage. I was relieved and knew that God had given me a second chance. I broke up with my boyfriend and decided I was going to change my life. I was invited by my ex-boyfriend's sister to a Wesleyan Holiness church in the city. I got baptized again and rededicated my life to the Lord.

Reflection

After rededicating my life to the Lord, my relationship with my mom got better, but I still felt distant from her. It was an unspoken feeling. One Thursday morning in June 2010, I received the tragic news from my sister that my mom had been found unconscious in her house by a neighbor and taken to the hospital. She had a reported temperature of 104°. My sister told me she looked very bad and might not make it. After hanging up, I started crying hysterically. I did not want my mom to die without getting the chance to let her know that I had forgiven her for not being there when I was growing up. I wanted to tell her that I missed not having her while growing up and that I loved her. I prayed that God wouldn't let her die.

Mom developed septicemia from an injury to her foot that became infected. After a long hospitalization, she survived, but she lost her memory. Eventually, since she had no one to care for her in St. Lucia, my sister took her in, and my mom now lives with her here in the United States. To my astonishment, my mom cannot remember who I am. Every time I visit her, I have to reintroduce myself to her, and when I walk away, I can feel the pain in my heart. I feel that I have been abandoned yet again. She also cannot remember anyone else, including my sister, but it's personal to me because of what she did to me when I was little. I never had my mom, and now it seems that I have lost her forever.

PART 2

Finding Love

Therefore a man shall leave his father and his mother and hold fast to his wife, and they shall become one flesh.

—Genesis 2:24

*I*t was 1978. I was seventeen years old, and on Sunday afternoons, my church group would go to the hospital to visit and pray for the sick. It was there that I met a young man who would later become my husband. As I introduced myself, it turned out that we had previously met in a church conference. His leg was in traction, and he could not move. He told me that he had been in a car accident and had suffered a broken leg. I visited him often and soon started falling in love with him. He was very charming and loving, and when I was with him, I felt something that I had never felt before. He had a beautiful voice and would sing to me while playing his guitar. He made me feel special. No one had ever made me feel this way before. I began to feel I could not live my life without him. After he was discharged from the hospital, he invited me to his parents' home. His folks were very nice and welcomed me with open arms.

For months I wanted to tell my mom about this young man I had met, with whom I had fallen madly in love, but I was afraid of her possible reaction. When I finally worked up the courage to tell her, she was hysterical. She told me that she was going to disown me and did not want to meet him.

This news caught me completely off guard because we had already made what we thought was a beautiful plan to introduce him. The plan was for the young man and his pastor to come and meet my mom and tell her of our love for each other. On the morning of the meeting, I had to wake up early to go to town and stop them from coming to see my mom. I longed for the type of love he and his family had shown me. After my mom's rejection of him, I told her that I would not stop seeing him, whether she liked it or not. We became inseparable, and about one year later, we got married.

It was November 10, 1979, a beautiful, sunny day. There I was at the age of eighteen, standing at the altar in a pink dress, saying my wedding vows.

"I, Gigi, take you to be my lawfully wedded husband, to have and to hold, from this day forward, for better or for worse, for richer or for poorer, in sickness and in health, until death do us part."

My mother, of course, did not attend the wedding. I was surrounded by his family and about ten people from our church. You may wonder why was I wearing pink. Someone had told me that, since I was not a virgin, I could not wear a white dress, and I just complied. I did not feel worthy enough to wear a white dress. I never told my husband about my sexual abuse, but its effects crawled into my marriage. For one, I was ashamed of my body;

for a long time after we got married, I could not be intimate with my husband unless the lights were out.

His parents asked us to move in with them while we saved up for a place of our own. After spending approximately five years with my mom, still longing for that motherly love, I left my mom's home to be with my husband.

We finally saved enough money for a place of our own, but approximately one year after we got married, Hurricane Allen, a Category 4 hurricane, struck St. Lucia. I remember this event as if it had occurred yesterday. The day before the hurricane struck was a calm Monday afternoon in November of 1980. I was on my way to the hospital to visit my husband, who was frequently hospitalized due to the motor vehicle accident he suffered earlier in his life. The dark clouds hovered over the horizon, and there was a sadness in the atmosphere ... a sadness that contradicted the joy of my heart. I was reminded of the earlier announcements about the pending hurricane. I thought that this must be the calm before the storm. Well, that night, while I cuddled in my husband's arms in his hospital bed, the heavens opened; the wind whistled as part of the hospital's roof flew away. Luckily, we were rescued by hospital personnel, who moved us to another part of the hospital. I remembered going home the next morning in astonishment. The house we were renting had been washed out to sea, and all our belongings had gone with it. Nearly everyone in the village had lost their houses, and some had even lost their lives, so I was grateful to be alive. With nowhere to turn and no place to live, I went to see if my mom was all right. I was relieved to find that her little, old house was standing when most of the newer houses around it were gone. It was a miracle that her house was left standing, and I was very happy that my mom, brother, and sister were all alive. My husband and I took refuge at her home.

Since my mom never approved of my husband, I was afraid of how she might react, but the tragedy of the hurricane seemed to have softened her heart. Living with my mom again in her one-bedroom house helped me form some type of mother-daughter bond, but I still could not relate to her. She also got to know my husband, and I felt she liked him.

Later that year, some missionaries came from America to build houses for those who had lost their homes. He and I were awarded a house, and soon we left my mom's home to move into our small but comfortable new home. I loved and respected my husband very much. I looked up to him. He was the leader of the young people in our church. He was involved in the youth choir and often preached when the pastor was absent.

The pastor of our church assigned him and me the task of conducting services every Sunday in a small section of our village. The town was about twenty minutes from our main church. Since we had to walk, I remember praying for a vehicle so our journey would not be so long. God answered our prayer, and we were able to purchase a van.

For once in my life, I felt loved and important and secure. He had a good sense of humor and made me laugh all the time. He was my idol, my hero, my ideal man. He and I had the perfect marriage ... or so I thought.

THE FIRST BETRAYAL

$\mathcal{T}$he perfect marriage lasted all of three years. I became pregnant with our son, and then my husband started changing. My husband started going out at night and returning the next morning, always giving me some excuse for being out all night. I remembered staying up all night and crying while wondering where he was. He stopped going to church, and I began hearing rumors of him having an affair. When I confronted him, he assured me that the rumors were false. He always assured me of his love. I was emotionally needy and needed to hear him say *I love you*, which he always said to me. Of course I believed he was genuine because I did not think he would ever betray our love. Our son was born on January 10, 1982. By then I was twenty-one and he was twenty-four.

Our relationship started deteriorating, yet I continued to deny the possibility that my husband had been unfaithful. Finally I found a sexually suggestive letter in his pocket. The letter was from a young woman. Then I started to believe that he really was cheating on me. I was devastated. My world had been shattered, and I felt physically sick. A mixture of emotions came upon me. I felt rage, uncertainty, shock, agitation, fear, unbearable pain, and confusion—all at the same time. How could he do this to me? What about the marriage vows we took? Did they not mean anything to him? I really did not know what to do. I could not tell my mom because I did not want her to have a bad image of him. The feelings of worthlessness and the absence of love that I had experienced for decades crept back into my life. I started to think that perhaps something was wrong with me. Why would he cheat? He assured me all the time how much he loved me and enjoyed being with me. I really felt his love and could not understand why this was happening. To make matters worse, his partner in adultery was one of the young women in the church. I felt so ashamed. Soon news of the affair started spreading all over the small village where we lived. We had been on the street corners so many times, preaching in open-air meetings, and people were talking about how he had been unfaithful even as he preached the gospel. The pastor, of course, took the assignment away from us.

In an angry outburst, I told my husband to leave the house; I could not leave with the baby. He left briefly and came back a few days later, begging for forgiveness. We made up, and this started a roller-coaster ride in our relationship that would last for years to come. I never felt the same toward him again. I no longer trusted him. I prayed every day for God to give me back the feeling I had for him, but my emotions were never the same after his infidelity.

Soon he told me we had to leave the village, probably because he was feeling ashamed. So we left the home that had been given to us, took all our belongings, and went to live in a rented property in the city. I guess he thought moving away from the village would give him a fresh start, but that did not happen.

My husband continued to backslide from the church and started having numerous affairs. Each time I found out about one of them, he would say he was sorry; I would forgive him, and the cycle continued. I had vowed to give my son the life I never had. I wanted him to have his daddy and mommy there for him. I believed my husband was going to change back into the loving and caring person he was when I first met him.

Reflection

Dealing with my emotions shortly after I discovered my husband's affair overshadowed everything else in my life. I felt sick to my stomach and found myself unable to concentrate on anything. It was very difficult for me to deal with the realization that my husband was cheating on me. It was extremely painful and cruel. I continued to hold onto hope that my marriage could survive my husband's cheating, but every time I thought about it, I felt sick inside. I just could not understand why he would do something like that.

COMING TO AMERICA

In June of 1982, my husband decided to go to the United States on vacation. When he arrived, he decided to stay and wanted my son and me to join him. While preparing to come to the States, I received a letter from a woman who claimed that she was pregnant by my husband. She warned me that I should not come to America because he was planning to divorce me and marry her. She said that she had been reading all my letters to him and that I should not waste my time because he loved her, not me. I was hysterical when I got her letter. All this time I had believed him when he told me he was going back to church, was trying to do right, and could not wait for us to be together as a family again. When I told him about the letter, he said that the girl's claims were lies, that she was living in an apartment they shared with three other people, and that he did not have a relationship with her. I believed him, wanting to give him the benefit of a doubt. So I paid no mind to this woman's words, and my son and I joined him in America in September of 1983.

We settled in Brooklyn, New York, and for a while, our lives went well. He had been attending a small Pentecostal storefront church, and its pastor had sent the invitation for my son and me to get our visas to come to the States. The pastor was very happy to meet us. My son was eighteen months old, and I was twenty-two by then. All was going well. The pastor was having my husband preach, but once again, his ministry was short-lived.

One Sunday morning, approximately one month after our arrival in America, a girl walked into the church service we were attending. I would learn that she was the woman who had written to me about this latest affair. She started shouting at me, saying that the two of them were having an affair. Everything came to a halt, and silence permeated the building; all eyes were on him and the woman. The pastor asked her to leave, but she refused. The whole congregation thought she was crazy until my husband confirmed that her claims were true. He admitted to the affair but claimed he had broken it off when I came to the States. He said she was not pleased with the breakup, and this was her way of getting back at him. He started apologizing to everyone, saying that he was very sorry. I was so embarrassed and ashamed that I left the service that morning, crying hysterically. Infidelity is difficult enough to deal with when only you and your spouse know about it; having multiple people know that your spouse cheated is catastrophic to your self-esteem. It is extremely humiliating and degrading.

One month later the pastor died. Dear Pastor Robinson died of a heart attack one Sunday morning while preparing to come to church. I often wondered if learning of my husband's infidelity had something to do with his death; he had been very disappointed after learning what he had done. The church closed after the pastor died, and we started going to another storefront church. Once again our marital life went well, but the peace only lasted for a while. He soon stopped going to church and started having numerous affairs. He started drinking and would often come home drunk. It was the summer of 1986, and we had yet another fight because I asked him to stop what he was doing. I found out he was dating yet another girl who claimed to be my friend and was always at our apartment. That night he almost strangled me to death. Thank God, I was rescued by a friend and her husband, who were visiting us.

SHATTERED DREAMS

(Baby on Board)

Up until this point in our marriage, there had been no solid evidence of my husband's unfaithfulness other than his confessions. Then, one evening in July of 1987, the phone rang, and I answered it. On the other end was a woman's voice, asking to speak to my husband. I told her he was not at home, and she proceeded to tell me that she needed urgently to get in touch with him because her sister was in the hospital in labor. Her sister was my friend and often came to my house. I wondered why she was calling him. I was dumbfounded as the details of this scenario came together. I could not believe it—my friend was having my husband's baby. I remember going to the bathroom and unrolling about twenty rolls of toilet paper and just sobbing. Sitting in a pool of toilet paper, I cried out to the Lord, "Why me? Why is my life so full of pain? What is wrong with him? I dealt with all of the previous affairs, but this time a baby? How will I deal with that? Dear Lord, help me, I pray."

When he came home that evening, I told him about the phone call and asked why. I did not have strength for another fight. He just said he was very sorry and claimed that he was not seeing her anymore but was planning on taking care of the baby.

Really? I thought. *You're not even taking care of us.*

I wanted to leave, but I had no family here in America, and I was not working. It finally struck me that I was not going to be able to give my son the life that I had promised him. I had to take action because my husband was not providing for us. We started getting eviction letters from the landlord, and he did not seem to care. I felt stuck because, instead of working, I was studying for the GED exam. Having passed, I enrolled in the nursing program at New York City Technical College in Brooklyn, New York.

Six months later, conditions were still the same. One Sunday, after returning home from church, I found my husband and his girlfriend in our living room with her baby. I felt so worthless that I wished the earth would open and swallow me up. How dare he! How could he bring his girlfriend into our home with no regard for me and how I'd feel about it? I told him to ask her to leave, and he did not respond fast enough, so I quickly asked her to leave.

"I will leave when he asks me to leave," she replied.

Stunned at her arrogance, I looked at my husband and said, "Please ask her to leave."

Finally he asked her to leave, but she then responded, "I will leave soon."

Not soon enough, I thought. I tried to remain calm but felt a mixture of anger and confusion. I knew I had to do something; I just didn't know what. I was thinking of my son, knowing that if I did anything crazy, I would go to prison. Who would take care of him then? But I had to do something to show them how angry I was. I proceeded to put a pan of water on the stove, making sure that it was only lukewarm, not hot enough to cause severe burns. When I felt it was warm enough, I took it into the living room and threw it on the girl. She jumped on me, and we started fighting right there in my living room. I still had my church suit and my high-heeled shoes on. Instead of breaking up the fight, my husband was charging at me to hit me. Then my friend Jen, who was living with us at the time, intervened and separated us. My husband's girlfriend left quickly with her child. I had ripped her clothes apart, so my husband gave her his shirt to put on and left with them.

I thought, *this is it! I have to leave this relationship.*

I had nowhere to go, so I called a friend, a woman I barely knew. I had met her in my college science class. I asked if I could stay with her. She told me I was welcome to stay, so I packed all my belongings from my three-bedroom apartment and asked another friend from the church to keep some items for me in her basement. When I arrived at my friend's home, she was nowhere to be found. I had a truck packed with my belongings and nowhere to put them, so I asked the driver to take the items, and I left. Thanks be to God that I can laugh at this now.

Unfortunately, this was not the end of the relationship between me and my husband. After I left the apartment, he ended up in the hospital, and I visited him a couple of times. I remember him telling me that he felt someone had pulled the rug out from under him. For some strange reason, I started feeling very sorry for him. I remember telling him that he needed to rededicate his life to the Lord and really repent of his ways. We got back together again and moved into another apartment. The three years I attended college were very difficult—amidst all the disruptions of my marriage, I had to stay focused on my studies.

The nursing program at New York City Technical College was extremely intense. I buried my head in my studies, realizing this was going to be the passport to take my son and me out of this relationship and into a better life. I can recall one course that was very hard, and everyone had failed it. Even after the professor decided to lower the passing mark, only three of us made it. I remember asking God to let me be among the ones to pass. I made all kinds of promises to God, telling him that I would go into the ministry if only he would let me pass, and he answered my prayer. I really thank God.

I graduated in June of 1990 with a GPA of 3.70. I received an associate's degree in nursing, passed the nursing board exam that July, and started work at Beth Israel Hospital in New York in August of that same year.

By that point, my husband's multiple affairs had produced two children by two different women. We separated and reconciled about six times during these three years. Something kept making me go back to this abusive and manipulative man. Believe it or not, even after all I had been through with him, deep down in my heart, I still loved him. I hated what he was doing and kept hoping that he would change, but each time his behavior only got worse.

Reflection

You may wonder why I stayed in such a relationship. Women stay with their cheating spouses for a number of reasons. I had stayed up to that point because I believed in the sanctity of my marriage vows: "For richer or for poorer, for better or for worse, in sickness and in health, till death do us part." I took these vows that I had made at the altar before God very seriously, and I wanted to fulfill them. Furthermore, Jesus tells us in Mark 10:9, (NIV) "Therefore what God has joined together, let no man separate." More than the vows spoken before my pastor, as a Christian, I believe that marriage represents the relationship of Christ to his church. The church is often referred to as the bride of Christ.

Secondly, I stayed because, despite the adulterous life my husband was living, I deeply loved him. This sounds crazy now, but I loved him so much that I would often wonder what I would do if he died and literally burst into tears at the thought. I was also afraid of being alone and was apprehensive about living without him. I was in my own little world, which consisted of myself, my son, and my husband. I could not discuss any of these problems with my mom or any other family member.

As I mentioned before, my husband was a very charming person, very jovial. He made me laugh all the time. Again, even if he was cheating, he made me feel special, and no one had made me feel this way before. Most of the time, after I found out about his affairs, he would admit guilt, say that he was sorry, and promise never to do it again. Then he would hold me in his arms, assuring me how much he loved me and our son and that he meant to change. I believed him each time, and I stayed because I truly believed he would change. I wanted my son to have the family I never had, a father and mother who would be there for him. He filled the void I had because I lacked a dad and, for the most part, had a mom who was not present while I was growing up.

In an article entitled "How To Cope When You've Learned Your Spouse Is Unfaithful" Sheri Stritof, marriage expert writes, "If your partner has cheated, you probably want to know why, but there is no simple answer to the question of why someone becomes unfaithful. It could be a symptom of other problems in the marriage. It could relate to something in your spouse's past. Or it could be totally unrelated to the other spouse or the marriage. You may never truly know why it happened." She gives the following advice:

1. Don't make any major decisions about ending your marriage immediately just because your spouse has been unfaithful. This is the time to do some reflection on your marriage to see what other issues, other than this infidelity, need to be recognized and addressed.

2. Feelings are neither right nor wrong. Accept that your feelings of rage, uncertainty, shock, agitation, fear, pain, depression, and confusion about having an unfaithful spouse are normal.

3. Take care of yourself. You may have some physical reactions to the infidelity: nausea, diarrhea, sleep problems (too little or too much), shakiness, difficulty concentrating, and decreased or excessive appetite.

4. Balance is the key to coping with infidelity. Force yourself to eat healthy foods, to stay on a schedule, to sleep regular hours, to get some exercise each day, to drink plenty of water, and to have some fun.

5. It's okay and healthy to laugh. Watch some funny movies or TV shows. Spend some time with people who make you smile. Life goes on in spite of heartache and unfaithful spouses.

6. Tears are healthy too. If they aren't coming naturally, put on some blues music or watch a sad movie. Those betrayed may actually feel numb, but it is important to get in touch with your underlying emotions as well.

7. Begin a journal. Write down your thoughts and feelings about your spouse's unfaithfulness.

8. Ask all the questions you want. Talk with your spouse about the infidelity. However, you may have to accept that your spouse may not know why the infidelity took place or may not want to reveal this to you.

9. Seek counseling. Don't try to cope with unfaithfulness alone. However, don't shout from the highest mountain that your spouse is an unfaithful jerk. Make careful choices of the people to whom you will confide this information. Knowing the type of infidelity sometimes makes understanding it easier, and counseling can help one to find answers to questions. Was it a one-night stand or an affair? Was it due to a midlife or personal crisis? Is it a sexual addiction or an act of retaliation? Did the cheating occur deliberately to end the marriage?

10. Take it one day at a time. Both you and your spouse should be tested for AIDS/HIV and STDs before you resume sexual intimacy without protection. Consider what boundaries you need in your marriage in order to stay in the marriage. Contact an attorney and get these documented in a postnuptial agreement.

11. Your children need to know that you are going to be okay. You can't hide the fact that you are going through a trauma. Be honest with your children, but don't weigh them down with details about how your spouse cheated on you. Don't make promises that you can't keep.

12. Try to avoid the blame game over who or what caused the infidelity. It's just wasted energy. That includes blaming the third party. It won't change anything. Also, think twice before telling your family or your spouse's family about the infidelity. Family members can often hold grudges for a very long time.

13. You may have post-traumatic stress. If you are jumpy, yell at trivial actions, feel like you are walking on egg shells, and continue to have physical reactions when you are reminded of the infidelity, see a physician as soon as you can. Medication even temporarily, might be a good idea.

14. It takes time to get beyond the pain of having an unfaithful mate. Don't expect the mixture of feelings, the sense of confusion and limbo, and the mistrust to go away just because you've tried to forgive your spouse and made a commitment to save your marriage. The stages of death and dying (denial, anger, bargaining, depression and acceptance) are part of the grieving process. It doesn't mean your marriage can't be renewed and strengthened, because it can. But, it will be different. Remember that your marriage has changed. You will need to grieve that loss.

15. Get Practical. Look at your finances, housing situation, transportation, etc. If you do decide to end your marriage, make sure you have enough money to pay for your essentials, etc. If you are unsure this the right decision, seek counseling as well to guide you.

The distinction between blaming yourself for your husband's affair and accepting responsibility for your part in the breakdown of the marriage is a crucial one. While you may have contributed to the problems in your relationship, the decision to cheat was your husband's, and his alone. His affair is not a reflection of your attractiveness or value as a wife, a lover, or a woman. Psychotherapist Barton Goldsmith advises readers, in the article "Ten Ways to Raise Your Self-Esteem," as follows. "Whenever you catch yourself having negative thoughts about yourself, stop yourself. Instead, consciously tell yourself something positive about yourself. Spend your energy on positive thoughts and pursuits, such as a hobby you enjoy, or exercise."

In an article entitled "What if your spouse cheats?" Dr. Gary D. Chapman points out, "When you married, you made a vow pledging your faithfulness. But now you've discovered your spouse didn't take that vow seriously. It doesn't matter whether it was a one - night stand or a long –term affair, the results are the same – your spouse actions has left in its wake fear, doubt, distrust, betrayal, hurt and anger. Ultimately, it's what you do with these emotions – how you process them –that makes the difference. For you and your marriage's sake you need to process these emotions in a positive way." He offers the following Healthy verses Un-heathy Responses:

- **Allow the tears to flow.** Initially, crying is a healthy response. But your body is limited to how long it can sustain such agony. Allow yourself to cry, but don't move into a "poor me" attitude. That will do no one any good.
- **Tell your spouse how you feel.** Verbally expressing your feelings is also a healthy way to process anger—as long as you use "I" statements rather than "you" statements.

When you say, "You betrayed me. You took advantage of me. You don't love me," you only incite negative reactions. And we know that negative reactions don't lead to positive outcomes.

Statements such as, "I feel betrayed. I feel hurt. I feel like you don't love me" simply reveal your emotions. They're honest and communicate the depth of your pain.

- **Control your behavior.** Negative responses to anger can complicate the problem. If you start throwing dishes or speaking obscenities, your out-of-control behavior will only alleviate your spouse's guilt. Now he can blame you rather than himself because your behavior has demonstrated that you're an unreasonable, uncontrolled person.

- **Don't retaliate.** Retaliation is a common but negative response. Vengeful tactics include having an affair yourself to show your unfaithful spouse what it feels like to be betrayed or going to her workplace to cause a scene. Any effort at revenge is .doomed to failure. Returning wrong for wrong simply makes the other person feel less guilty and stimulates him or her to return fire for fire.

- **Seek outside help.** After the initial wave of shock, hurt, and anger, the most productive step you can take is to seek the wisdom of a Christian counselor. If your spouse isn't willing to go, then go alone. You're more likely to make wise decisions if you get the help of someone who isn't emotionally involved in the situation.

Accept Your Feelings

Instead of beating yourself up for how you are feeling, acknowledge and accept your feelings. You may be hurt, confused, or lonely. Tell yourself that these are perfectly natural emotions to experience after a betrayal. Treat yourself with kindness and care and take the time to explore your feelings further rather than pushing them away. In an article for the *Huffington Post*, relationship expert Margaret Paul points out that painful, difficult feelings can draw your attention to your needs; taking steps to meet those needs, once you recognize them, will make you feel loved and boost your confidence.

PART 3

Finding the Strength Within

He gives strength to the weary, and to him who
has no might he increases power. Do not fear, for I
am with you; do not be afraid, for I am your God.
I will strengthen you, be assured I will help you; I
will certainly take hold of you with my righteous
right hand.

—Isaiah 40:29; 41:10 (AMP)

In November of 1990, my husband and I were reconciling for
about the seventh time. Yet again he had convinced me that he
had changed and wanted his family to be together; like a fool, I
gave in again. We decided to move to another part of the state for
a fresh start. We found an apartment and decided to settle down,
and once again our lives seemingly went well for a while. He
started going back to church, but it was soon becoming a vicious
cycle, and I continued to fall into it. The two of us decided that
we should have another child, and I became pregnant in January
of 1993. We had saved enough money to purchase a home, and
in April of 1993, we bought a two-family home.

Once again, changing our location failed to make a difference. As soon as he felt comfortable in our relationship, he would start cheating again. He always said he was sorry, but he never truly repented. By the time my daughter was born, relations between us had started getting really bad. He started coming home drunk at night, and his cheating continued. My precious daughter was born on October 13, 1993, and by then my son was twelve.

On several occasions, my husband's women were calling my home and looking for him, which led to several arguments. Once again he stopped going to church. By that point, I realized that the problem was with him. You would think that I would have realized that a long time ago, but instead I had kept asking myself what was wrong with me. He had some inadequacy in him, and I certainly was not going to be able to help him.

I decided that I was not going to continue living a lie. I started hating what he was doing to me: the cheating, the lying, the drinking, and the constant fighting. I started asking myself why I had allowed him to torture me like this. How about my children? Was this the kind of relationship I wanted them to have? Why did I constantly allow him back in my life when I knew that he would never change? What was wrong with me? I had remained a devoted Christian and gotten the strength from God to be able to stay in this relationship. I started questioning my faith in God. I felt that I was being punished for some sin that I had committed.

One evening, after a night of drinking, my husband started arguing with me. He got very upset and went on a rampage, breaking all the furniture in the house. I stood there, screaming, with my daughter, then six months old, in my arms, trying to comprehend what was going on. This was a monster that I had never seen before, and I knew it was time to get out of that relationship for good. I started having flashbacks of the time he almost strangled me. Feeling simultaneously helpless and angry, I started brainstorming about what I was going to do. Suddenly the emotional abuse I had suffered throughout the years began taking a toll on me. I thought of divorce, but the words in Malachi 2:16 echoed through my mind—"I hate Divorce says the Lord God of Israel."

I started thinking and praying that he would die so that I would not have to go through a divorce. When it appeared that God was not going to answer my prayers, I decided to take matters into my own hands and starting having thoughts of what I could do to take his life. Once again I remembered the words of the sixth commandment, "Thou shalt not kill." I felt trapped. I did not know what to do. All I knew was that I could not go on living like this any longer.

That evening, with tears in my eyes and pain in my heart, I made the toughest decision I ever had to make and called the police to have them arrest my husband for domestic violence. I cried because I had finally realized that I could not have the loving family I had yearned for as a child and promised to give my children. I got a permanent restraining order against my husband. I wish there had been a better ending to my saga, one fitting the vow we took "for better or for worse … till death do us part." Our outcome would not be like that. Securing that restraining order was the hardest action I had had to take. After praying and reading, I found the grace to file for divorce six years after this last breakup. Yet he was not giving up, and after seventeen years of marriage, he still tried to tell me that he would change and that he loved me. He then tried to cast the blame on me, telling me to look at what I was doing to the family and that I was the one breaking us apart. I was determined not to let him back into my life, so I started counseling, which helped me a great deal.

For many years I struggled with forgiving my husband. As a Christian, I struggled with guilt and shame because my marriage did not work and ended in divorce. I became resentful of my husband for the physical and emotional abuse I had suffered. I regretted spending seventeen years of my life in misery with him. I was very angry that I was left to take care of the children, mortgage, and other responsibilities.

From 1994 to 2004, my relationship with God was not great. I was too preoccupied with working two jobs while also going to school to further my nursing career, eventually completing my bachelor's degree in nursing. I went to church every other Sunday when I was not working, and that was it. My everyday prayer was, "Dear Lord, please protect me from sickness and keep me safe so I can continue working to take care of my children." I did not get involved in any church activities because I did not have the time. I was too busy just trying to survive, failing to realize that the Lord was giving me the strength to endure my hardships.

I felt overwhelmed at times by the pressures of working two jobs, going to school, and trying to care for my two children. I remember walking through the house, crying and asking God why my life had been so miserable. I would continue to miss my husband at times, in spite of everything he had put me through, and wonder why he could not change.

I had made up my mind that I was destined to be alone the rest of my life. But then, nine years after my divorce, I met someone and decided to give love another chance. I was attracted to this person because he told me he was a pastor and that we would do ministry together. He rather reminded me of my first husband. He had a passion for the Lord, he was well versed in the Bible, and he was a prayer warrior.

With all this in mind, when he asked me to marry him, I was very excited and enthusiastically said, "Yes!" I thought I was getting a second chance, but little did I know the pain I was about to endure. I think it is every woman's dream to walk down the aisle dressed in white. I was mesmerized by the thought of getting married again.

This time I said to myself, "It's going to be the wedding I never had." So I went all out with bridesmaids and groomsmen. We also had a beautiful reception and a wonderful honeymoon. And, most importantly to me, my mom was present. Thinking about it now, I realized that I had fallen in love with the idea of a marriage ceremony rather than the groom. This fixation caused me to ignore every warning sign not to marry this person. I shut my eyes and closed my ears to the potential problems I was seeing and hearing. I failed to ask the hard questions when his attitude and his behaviors looked suspicious to me. For example, we were out on a date one day. While I was driving he ducked suddenly, hiding himself inside the car. When I questioned him about his behaviour, he stated that he was hiding from someone he knew - this was a red flag I ignored. I guess I was still yearning for an intact family with a husband present.

All I wanted was to get married and have the wedding that I never had. Even during marriage counseling, I ignored certain facts about that person. I remarried in June of 2006 at the age of forty-five. Soon after the wedding, the emotional abuse started. My spouse made attempts to isolate me from my family. I was accused of being unfaithful and of having an abortion simply because I was going through menopause and my periods were irregular. If the pastor gave me an assignment at church, like teaching a Sunday school class, for instance, he would get very angry at me, stating that the pastor should have asked him for permission first. I didn't know if his beliefs were cultural or not, but I was still dumbfounded by his logic. This clash between our mindsets would lead us to argue for days. I was constantly criticized about my weight and called names like "ganger bear." I did not know what that meant, but it sounded like a big bear to me. I did not consider myself overweight. At five feet, eight and a quarter inches, I weighed a hundred and eighty pounds and wore a size twelve. But as a result of his critical and negative comments, I started believing that I was fat like a big bear. I started an exercise regime and lost about twenty pounds, but that still did not make my husband happy. I was also told what and what not to wear.

My second spouse constantly made attempts to control me. I did my best to be a submissive wife, but nothing I did was good enough. We attempted counseling, but that did not help because my husband failed to take responsibility for any wrongdoing in our relationship. If the counselor did not agree with him, he said the counselor was no good. I started questioning the poor choice I had made, which brought me to the realization that I had failed to seek God's will for this marriage. I cried out to the Lord and asked for his forgiveness.

One of the courses available at my church was "Finding Your Place in the Ministry." Taking this course made me realize my calling to the counseling ministry. I started using what I was learning to help my marriage, but my efforts did not seem to help. I started feeling very anxious because I did not know how to please my husband. I became very unhappy, angry, and bitter. I was turning into a different person, and I did not like the person I was turning into. Strangely, I was unable to apply any of the material I was learning to my marriage. I could not understand how this person, a prayer warrior and Christian who knew the

Bible from Genesis to Revelation, could have such a negative and hurtful personality.

There were constant quarrels and heated arguments. I did not trust him. After we married, I learned that my husband had been married before in his country of origin but had failed to disclose that fact to me. Technically I was his third wife, not his first. He also had a second wife, of whom I knew, but he had not told me about his first wife. Many times I felt that I was sleeping with the enemy, and I knew there was no way I could stay in such a marriage. By then I had finished my master's degree and was working on my doctorate in Christian counseling. The emotional and verbal abuse continued, and this marriage also came to an end after an episode of domestic violence.

His seventeen-year-old son had just arrived here from another country, and I witnessed him ruthlessly beating his son for no apparent reason. The picture of violence from my previous marriage flashed before my eyes. I expected to be the next target of his violence. When he became violent, I saw a side of him that I had never seen before, and I became very scared.

Beating his son was the cracking straw. I called the police. I was astonished to see him lie to the police and make his son lie, saying that he did not hit him, even though his son had multiple bruises to prove it. I looked into his son's eyes and saw utter terror. I was also extremely fearful. That same day, I asked my husband to leave because I could no longer continue living in this marriage. The marriage had lasted for four years.

After we separated, I started evaluating my life. I realized that I had made a poor choice in marrying this person. I started feeling very guilty that my second marriage had ended in failure. I could not forgive myself for making such poor decisions. I felt that I knew better.

As I continued to study, I realized that, for God to use me in my counseling ministry, I had to learn to forgive myself and the others who had hurt me, and so I began my journey of forgiveness.

THE PATH TO FORGIVENESS

Not to forgive is to be imprisoned by the past, by old grievances that do not permit life to proceed with new business. Not to forgive is to yield oneself to another's control ... to be locked into a sequence of act and response, of outrage and revenge, tit for tat, escalating always. The present is endlessly overwhelmed and devoured by the past. Forgiveness frees the forgiver. It extracts the forgiver from someone else's nightmare.

—Lance Morrow

But if you do not forgive others their trespasses, neither will your Father forgive your trespasses.

—Matthew 6: 15, ESV

In my first marriage, there were times when I told my husband I had forgiven him, but in my inmost heart, I remained bitter even almost thirteen years after the divorce. How could I truly forgive him after he had totally ruined my youth? How could I forgive him for choosing to live an adulterous life rather than being a loving and caring husband and father? How could I forgive him for all the pain he caused me? And how about my second husband? How could I forgive him for all the lies he told me and the mental and emotional abuse I had endured?

And what about all the perpetrators who sexually abused me for all those years? How could I forgive them? What about my mom? Could I ever forgive her for leaving me behind? How about myself? How could I forgive myself for all the poor choices I had made up to this point in my life? I was very disappointed in myself. I was feeling guilty, full of shame and remorse. First I had to receive God's forgiveness and his love for me, and then come to the realization that forgiving through one's own effort alone is impossible.

Forgiveness was initiated by God, embodied in Christ's blood, and empowered through the Holy Spirit. I began by asking God to work through me and to give me the willingness and the ability to walk through the process of forgiving myself. I made a list of specific hurts that were committed against me and listed the actions that affected me. I then claimed the truth that my life belongs to the Lord. I can now thank God for his forgiveness toward me, and I thank him for forgiving the offenders through me. I wrote letters to everyone who had hurt me, telling them how much they had hurt me, but then I went on to tell them that I had forgiven them. I then destroyed the letters without mailing them, passing all these sins to the cross. Since God has already paid the price for their offenses, I passed God's forgiveness on to all my offenders. Then I released the responsibility for punishment to God. After going through this process, I felt as light as a feather. I could feel the burden lifted off my shoulders. No more shame, no more blame, no more condemnation. I felt free.

Reflection

Forgiveness is difficult because it feels like letting the culprit off the hook, but one forgives the person, not the action. Forgiveness doesn't mean you weren't injured or that your misery has subsided. Nor is it a haughty, superior attitude. Forgiving is a decision to reclaim control of your life by refusing to lug around the agony of divorce any longer. It's reducing the offending person to a neutral factor—someone whose influence over you will diminish over time. Forgiving is easier if you start by asking God to forgive you. Even if you did nothing to cause your divorce or any of the hurt, you surely feel remorse for any disappointment or hurt you inadvertently caused. Realizing you need forgiveness and desiring it elevates your spiritual growth to a new level. It frees you from the need to be perfect as you honor the dignity of the offending person as a child of God. It makes you a better person. Don't misunderstand: Forgiveness doesn't mean you have to forget. If someone has sinned against you, you don't have to be foolish and set yourself up for more pain or abuse. It does mean that, in God's power, you free your transgressor from all your condemnation and judgment and choose to love that person, faults and all. In Romans 12:19 (NIV) we read, Do not take revenge, my dear friends, but leave room for God's wrath, for it is written: "It is mine to avenge; I will repay," says the Lord.

PART 4

Brokenness to Wholeness

Success is determined not by whether or not you face obstacles, but by your reaction to them. And if you look at these obstacles as a containing fence, they become your excuse for failure. If you look at them as a hurdle, each one strengthens you for the next.

—Ben Carson, *Gifted Hands:*
The Ben Carson Story

You have turned for me my mourning into dancing; you have loosed my sackcloth and clothed me with gladness, to the end that *my* glory may sing praise to you and not be silent. O Lord my God, I will give thanks to you forever.

—Psalm 30:11–12, NKJV

*Y*es, I was a broken human being. My spirit and soul were broken because of the circumstances that started back in my childhood days. I had suffered sexual abuse, felt unloved, and counted two failed marriages. Yes, I was broken, and brokenness hurts! I felt insignificant, empty, bitter, and ashamed. I felt alone and isolated. I walked around every day with a mask, pretending that everything was okay when I was practically dying on the inside with pain. And yet I was a born-again believer.

All over the world, people attempt to overcome pain by filling their lives with substitutes. These substitutes include alcohol, drugs, sex, material things, and even work. The main reason for taking these substitutes is to numb the pain by replacing it with something else. Usually people hope to avoid pain with these substitutes. However, most of them only serve to increase these feelings of brokenness and hopelessness, leading to lower self-esteem. Even as Christians, we are sometimes afraid to tell our fellow Christians the difficulties we are undergoing or the pain we are feeling for fear of being judged and condemned. This causes us to keep everything inside, allowing these hurts to fester and become open wounds. A wound that is not properly treated will get worse and worse until the whole body becomes infected and the patient develops septicemia. A septic soul is a lost and confused soul if we do not seek out the Lord.

As I began to understand who I was in Christ, I was filled with the blessed knowledge that I am loved, accepted, redeemed, forgiven, and freed from the law of sin and death. I am his workmanship, created in Christ Jesus, for good works. I am anointed. I am sanctified. I began to feel an inner power that I had never felt before. I began to feel his peace, the peace that passes all understanding. It was then that I saw my life as it had been and started looking for the good in the midst of all the bad that had happened to me. I knew that God had a purpose for my life. If we attempt to lift ourselves out of brokenness and become whole without turning to God, we will fail. We may improve our lot, but complete wholeness is not possible. We must turn to our Creator for help. He alone has the complete answer for us and the power to heal us.

WHOLENESS THROUGH CHRIST

$\mathcal{W}$e should strive for wholeness. We should be whole in body, soul, and spirit, but we cannot achieve this wholeness on our own. To be whole, we first have to be reconciled to God through Christ. Christ died for our sins upon the cross. As we believe in him and follow his teachings, he can help us deal with our brokenness and make us whole. For me, one of the greatest keys to experiencing wholeness is the peace of God. Peace is more than just experiencing outer circumstances of quietness and tranquility. It's experiencing inner quietness and tranquility even when circumstances go awry.

In John 10:10b, (KJV) Jesus said, "I came that they might have life, and that they might have it more abundantly." Here Jesus stated his primary goal for our lives. He wants us to have abundant lives. This abundant life does not always shield us from brokenness, but it will help us through the dark seasons and give us victory. In Psalm 147:3, (NIV) the psalmist wrote, "He heals the brokenhearted, and binds up their wounds." Jesus is always present to treat our wounds and heal our suffering hearts. He will give us abundant life! Therefore, to overcome our brokenness, we must realize that we have to be healed by a power greater than ourselves. If we only look to ourselves, we will not be able to travel from brokenness to wholeness. We choose what to do with our hurt. Jesus will not impose his healing upon us. We must make the decision to turn to him for healing.

Even in times of great testing, God is with us. According to Psalm 34:18, (NIV) "The Lord is near to the brokenhearted, and saves those who are crushed in spirit." This assertion gives us great hope. Even the darkest hours can be moments of peak fellowship with the eternal God. Our Lord will heal our crushed hearts.

Dr. Richard Swenson writes about the healing of broken relationships. He states, "Although there is no formula, there are principles. It helps to bring God close—through our brokenness. And it helps to accept God's grace—through our humility." Through brokenness and humility, with God nearby, our broken relationships can be healed.

Moreover, when people have experienced brokenness, they often minister more effectively. People who have been healed from brokenness can identify with those who are broken. We do not seek to be broken, but when we are, God can use it for his glory. Someone once said, "If you succeed without suffering, it is only because someone else suffered without succeeding."

God desires that we may be completely whole in every area of our lives. First Thessalonians 5:23–24 (MSG) states, "May God himself, the God who makes everything holy and whole, make you holy and whole, put you together—spirit, soul, and body— and keep you fit for the coming of our Master, Jesus Christ. The one who called you is completely dependable. If he said it, he'll do it."

Reflection

We need to realize that our circumstances are not an indication of whether God is with us or not. We Christians sometimes fall into the error of thinking that when our lives and plans are going well, it means that God must be with us, but when our world falls apart, God has abandoned us. Nothing could be further from the truth. Firstly, the Bible assures us that God will never leave us or forsake us. Secondly, it tells us that we will certainly face trials but that God will use these for good in our lives. He will comfort us in and through them. Several scriptural texts convey this commitment.

James 1:2–4: (NIV) "Consider it pure joy, my brothers and sisters, whenever you face trials of many kinds, because you know that the testing of your faith develops perseverance. Perseverance must finish its work so that you may be mature and complete, not lacking anything."

Romans 8:28: (NIV) "And we know that in all things God works for the good of those who love him, who have been called according to his purpose."

1 Peter 5:7: (NIV) "Cast all your anxiety on him because he cares for you."

CONCLUSION

*G*od has given me a special sensitivity to people in pain and he is using all my bad experiences for his good. I truly believe each of these events happened to me for a reason because God knows every detail and every moment in my life. Before I was born, he knew the struggles I would undergo. It's true that God does not waste a hurt. At the time, I could not understand why God was allowing this evil to happen to me, but I can see now how God is allowing me to use my experiences to help others. Having obtained a PhD in clinical Christian counseling, I have a counseling ministry and serve in my local church as its Christian counselor. I thank God every day for giving me the opportunity to serve in that capacity. Because of his power and grace, I can now thank him for every part of my life and genuinely proclaim that I would not change how I grew up, even if I could.

These experiences could have destroyed me, especially when I was at my grandmother's house, but because of God's grace, mercy, and protection, I was able to rise above all these circumstances and obtain victory. I am much stronger and more confident, and my faith in God is much stronger now.

My trials, struggles, and heartaches have enabled me to be the ministry leader for Celebrate Recovery in my church. It is a Christ-centered ministry based on twelve steps and eight recovery principles for people with all types of hurts, habits, and hang-ups. When I started this ministry four years ago, as of the writing of this book, an explosion went off in my spirit, and everything that had happened in my life began to make sense. In addition to helping others, I understood even better why God allowed the horrific events detailed in this book to happen to me. God knew I would minister to hurting people one day, and to do so more effectively, I would need to go into the fire to be refined for the master's use.

As I look back, I feel blessed, knowing that I have two beautiful children. My son is now an adult, and my daughter is a senior in college. It has not been easy to care and provide for them. I did everything that I could. Sometimes I worked both day and night, and I refinanced my home to fund their education. Despite being raised in poverty, I was able to send both of them to private schools and college. It has been and still is a struggle as I continue to support my daughter's education. I never let them know about the struggles or how hard I had to work to make sure they wanted for nothing. I did not want them to have any worries—in part because I felt guilty for the divorce and because they had only one parent while growing up. However, we are surviving, and it's all by the grace of God.

There were times when I wanted to give up, but each night, as I went to bed, I would think about my children, and these thoughts gave me the strength to keep going. I recall a time when I was sick and had to be admitted to the hospital for gallbladder surgery when my son was about thirteen. As I was being wheeled to the operating room, he held my hands and said, "Mommy, please don't leave us." I could see the fear in his eyes. Through my own tears, I promised him that I would not leave them and that I would be all right after the surgery. After the surgery I was unable to work for two months and had to move into the basement of my home while renting out the first and second floors to cover my mortgage. Yet God always provided for us until I was able to go back to work.

I love my children so very much, and I try to express and demonstrate my love to them, especially my daughter. Through my studies, I know that a father's willful negligence almost always creates a father-love deprivation in the daughter, and this lack manifests itself as "father hunger." Depending on the child's temperament, this deprivation can affect her in many ways. Not having those needs met by a father can create isolation and anger that can spill over into every other male relationship in a girl's life. I know that I cannot take the place of her father, as my son once told me, but having one parent show her love is better than none. So I try my best to tell her often that she is loved, beautiful, smart, and talented, and that God has a purpose and a plan for her life.

Throughout my life, I have shed enough tears to fill the Nile River. But thanks be to God for the message of Psalm 30:5b: (NIV) "Weeping may stay for the night but rejoicing comes in the morning." I know there are others who have gone through worse experiences, but each person's story is unique. My hope is that as you read my story, you will find hope, encouragement, and healing.

Those who have been left behind or abandoned by their parents may never know the reason such decisions were made. Sometimes it's for the better outcome and sometimes not. But we are to take comfort in knowing that our heavenly Father will never leave us or forsake us and will always watch over us.

For all of those who have been sexually abused, it is important to know that the abuse was not your fault, and you did not cause it in any way. I know that humiliation, shame, and fear can cause you to be silent, but you must find the courage to tell someone or share your story. Know that if you seek the Lord, he can heal the wounds of sexual abuse.

For those who have had failed marriages because of the infidelity of their spouses, know that there is hope. Your marriage does not have to end in divorce. Let divorce be a last resort. Seek counseling but also seek the Lord. Seeking the Lord is the most important effort. The Lord has said that he hates divorce for a reason.

Marriage is a picture of the covenant God has with his people (Hebrews 9:15). A covenant is an unbreakable commitment, and God wants us to understand how serious it is. When we divorce someone with whom we made a covenant, we perjure ourselves with the vow we made, and it makes a mockery of the God-created concept of covenant relationship.

God's design for the family was that one man and one woman should commit themselves to each other for life and rear children to understand the concept of this covenant. Children reared in a healthy, two-parent home have a far greater likelihood of establishing successful marriages themselves. In addition, studies have shown that those in two-parent homes are far less likely to live in poverty.

When Jesus was asked why the law permitted divorce, he responded that God only allowed it "because of the hardness of your hearts but from the beginning it was not so," as written in Matthew 19:8. God never intended divorce to be part of the human experience, and it grieves him when we harden our hearts and break a covenant that he created. Divorce feels like having a piece of yourself ripped away, which makes it very painful for both parties as well as the children. The aggrieved partners in a divorce are in pain from their broken relationships and feel betrayed by their spouses. Divorce stings, and it can leave lasting scars.

If your marriage has to end in divorce, as mine did, rest assured that the sin of divorce can be forgiven and that our God gives second chances. With his help, you can endure. You are not a second-class citizen.

If you are contemplating remarriage, please be very careful to seek the Lord's will about the person, especially if you have children. Those who remarry often have unrealistic expectations. They are in love and don't really understand that the replacement of a missing partner after divorce, desertion, or even death doesn't restore the family to its original status. On the contrary, remarriage will present them with a number of unanticipated issues such as the children's feelings of conflict over loyalty, the breakdown of parenting tasks, and the combination of disparate family cultures. I had to deal with all the above, and it can become a very daunting task.

We can rise above our difficult situations and become better by first and foremost recognizing and acknowledging that we are not always victims but rather active players and creators of our playing field. We need to seek and accept God's forgiveness, then pass it along by forgiving those who have hurt us, and then turn our circumstances over to the Lord. In Psalm 34:19 (AMP) we read, "Many hardships and perplexing circumstances confront the righteous, But the Lord rescues him from them all."

RESOURCES

My people are destroyed for lack of knowledge.
—Hosea 4:6a (KJV)

*C*hild sexual abuse is shrouded in secrecy and abetted by shame. While most abuse is hidden and up-to-date statistics are scarce, it is known that nearly 150 million girls and 73 million boys under 18 around the world have experienced forced sexual intercourse or other forms of sexual violence worldwide.

Here are some devastating statistics on child sexual abuse.

Sexual abuse in the Caribbean

In an article entitle "Fighting child sexual abuse in the Caribbean" Tamar Hahn writes, "In the Caribbean region, sexual violence against children is greatly underreported, and this abuse is often culturally sanctioned. A study in Jamaica indicated that men often believe they have a right to engage in sex with girls under their care, while children in Guyana reported believing that sexual violence can be blamed on a victim's clothing. Sexual violence against boys is especially underreported, and in some countries, is not even recognized as a crime."

"Sexual abuse happens everywhere – at home, school and in other institutions, and has a serious physical, psychological and social impact, not only on girls and boys, but also on the fabric of society. It is one of the main factors that contribute to HIV infections, and that is why it is not surprising that this region has one of the highest prevalence of HIV and AIDS worldwide," said Nadine Perrault, UNICEF Regional Child Protection Adviser for Latin America and the Caribbean. "Our experiences in preventing and responding to sexual abuse have taught us that laws by themselves have been ineffective in protecting children, mainly because of the silence surrounding the issue and the risks that victims face in speaking out – risks such as stigma, shame, harm and further violence. And then, often, children do not know where to turn."

Child Sexual Abuse Statistics

According to the National Center for Victims of Crime, the prevalence of child sexual abuse is difficult to determine because it is often not reported; experts agree that the incidence is far greater than what is reported to authorities. CSA is also not uniformly defined, so statistics may vary. Statistics below represent some of the research done on child sexual abuse.

The US Department of Health and Human Services Children's Bureau report, *Child Maltreatment 2010,* found that 9.2 percent of victimized children were sexually assaulted.

Studies by David Finkelhor, Director of the Crimes Against Children Research Center, show the following.

- One in five girls and one in twenty boys is a victim of child sexual abuse.

- Self-report studies show that twenty present of adult females and 5–10 percent of adult males recall a childhood sexual assault or sexual abuse incident.
- During a one-year period in the US, 16 percent of youths aged fourteen to seventeen had been sexually victimized.
- Over their lifetimes, 28 percent of US youths aged fourteen to seventeen had been sexually victimized.
- Children are most vulnerable to CSA between the ages of seven and thirteen.

According to a 2003 National Institute of Justice report, three out of four adolescents who have been sexually assaulted were victimized by someone they knew well.

A Bureau of Justice Statistics report shows that 1.6 percent (sixteen out of one thousand) of children between the ages of twelve and seventeen were victims of rape/sexual assault.

A study conducted in 1986 found that 63 percent of women who had suffered sexual abuse by a family member also reported a rape or attempted rape after the age of fourteen. Recent studies in 2000, 2002, and 2005 have all concluded with similar results.

Children who had an experience of rape or attempted rape in their adolescent years were 13.7 times more likely to experience rape or attempted rape in their first year of college.

A child who is the victim of prolonged sexual abuse usually develops low self-esteem, a feeling of worthlessness, and an abnormal or distorted view of sex. The child may become withdrawn and mistrustful of adults and can become suicidal.

Children who do not live with both parents, as well as children living in homes marked by parental discord, divorce, or domestic violence, have a higher risk of being sexually abused

In the vast majority of cases where there is credible evidence that a child has been penetrated, only between 5 and 15 percent of those children will have genital injuries consistent with sexual abuse.

Child sexual abuse is not solely restricted to physical contact; such abuse could include noncontact abuse such as voyeurism and child pornography.

Compared to those with no history of sexual abuse, young males who were sexually abused were five times more likely to cause teen pregnancy, three times more likely to have multiple sexual partners, and two times more likely to have unprotected sex, according to the study published online and in the March 2012 print issue of the *Journal of Adolescent Health*.

Statistics on Perpetrators of Child Sexual Abuse

- Offenders are overwhelmingly male, ranging from adolescents to the elderly Some perpetrators are female. It is estimated that women are the abusers in about 14 percent of cases reported among boys and 6 percent of cases reported among girls.
- Approximately one-third of offenders are themselves juveniles.
- Individuals under the age of eighteen are the perpetrators in 23 percent of reported cases of child sexual abuse.
- Only 14 percent of children who suffered sexual abuse were violated by an unknown perpetrator.
- In the cases of 60 percent of children who are sexually abused, the abuser is someone in their social circle. Hence, the phrase "stranger danger" is misleading

- Meta-analysis estimates that 14 percent of sexual offenders commit another sexual offense after five years; 24 percent commit another sexual offense after fifteen years.
- *Child Maltreatment 2010* reports that 6.2 percent of child abusers sexually abused a child.
- Between 40 and 80 percent of juvenile sex offenders have themselves been victims of sexual abuse (*Advances in Clinical Child Psychology*, page 19).

Statistics on Disclosing Child Sexual Abuse

- Of the children victimized in 2011, 13 percent had at least one victimization known to police, while 46 percent had one known to school, police, or medical authorities.
- In contrast to the 13 percent of victimizations known to police and 2 percent known to medical professionals, 42 percent of school officials knew about victimization episodes.
- Most commonly, authorities knew about more serious victimizations, such as sexual assault by a known adult (69 percent) or unspecified adult (76 percent).
- The Office of Juvenile Justice and Delinquency Programs (OJJDP) found that authorities were least likely to know about victimizations that juveniles' peers were most likely to commit, such as flashing (17 percent) and completed and attempted rape (14 percent).
- In "Child and Youth Victimization Known to Police, School, and Medical Authorities," school authorities were the officials most likely to know about past-year victimization events—42 percent of victims had a victimization known to school authorities.

- Unlike school officials, many medical professionals were unaware of episodes of victimizations. Only 7 percent were aware of sexual abuse by a known adult, and 19 percent knew of sexual abuses by unknown adults.
- In fact, the recent study performed by OJJDP found that "school officials were more likely to know of sexual victimizations that occurred in school, were committed by an unidentified perpetrator, occurred to a child victim between 2 and 9 years old, or occurred to a child who lived with a stepparent or an unmarried partner of a parent."

Disclosure among Victims

- Not all sexually abused children exhibit symptoms—some estimate that up to 40% of sexually abused children are asymptomatic; however, others experience serious and long-standing consequences.
- A common presumption is that children will give one detailed, clear account of abuse. This is not consistent with research; disclosures often unfold gradually and may be presented in a series of hints. Children might imply something has happened to them without directly stating they were sexually abused—they may be testing the reaction to their "hint."
- If they are ready, children may then follow with a larger hint if they think it will be handled well.
- It is easy to miss hints of disclosure of abuse. As a result, a child may not receive the help needed.
- Disclosure of sexual abuse is often delayed; children often avoid telling because they are either afraid of a negative reaction from their parents or of being harmed

by the abuser. As such, they often delay disclosure until adulthood.

- Males tend not to report their victimization, which may affect statistics. Some men even feel societal pressure to be proud of early sexual activity, regardless of whether it was unwanted.
- Studies of adults suggest that factors such as the relationship to the perpetrator, age at first incident of abuse, use of physical force, severity of abuse, and demographic variables, such as gender and ethnicity, impact a child's willingness to disclose abuse.

When children do disclose:

- It is frequently to a friend or a sibling.
- Of all other family members, mothers are most likely to be told. Whether or not a mother might be told will depend on the child's expected response from the mother.
- Few disclose abuse to authorities or professionals.
- Of all professionals, teachers are the most likely to be told.
- Historically, professionals promoted the idea that children frequently report false accounts of abuse. Current research, however, lacks systematic evidence that false allegations are common. Recantations of abuse are also uncommon.

Resources for Child Abuse/Sexual Abuse

- National Child Abuse Hotline: They can provide local referrals for services. A centralized call center provides the caller with the option of talking to a counselor. They are also connected to a language line that can provide service in over 140 languages. Hotline: 800.4.A.CHILD (422.2253)

- Darkness to Light: They provide crisis intervention and referral services to children or people affected by sexual abuse of children. Hotline calls are automatically routed to a local center. Helpline: 866.FOR.LIGHT (367.5444)
- Cyber Tipline: This Tipline is operated by the National Center for Missing and Exploited Children. Can be used to communicate information to the authorities about child pornography or child sex trafficking. Hotline: 800. THE.LOST (843.5678)
- National Children's Alliance: This organization represents the national network of Child Advocacy Centers (CAC). CACs are a multidisciplinary team of law enforcement, mental and physical health practitioners who investigate instances of child physical and sexual abuse. Their website explains the process and has a directory according to geographic location.
- Stop It Now: Provides information to victims and parents/relatives/friends of child sexual abuse. The site has resources for offender treatment as well as information on recognizing the signs of child sexual abuse. Hotline: 888-PREVENT (773.8368)
- Justice for Children: Provides a full range of advocacy services for abused and neglected

Online supports for survivors of sexual abuse, including free and facilitated online support groups

http:www.stopitnow.org/help-guidance/online-help-center/adult-national

Sexual Assault Hotline - 1.800.656.HOPE

Survivors of Incest Anonymous http://www.siawso.org

Provides support and resources for anyone who has been affected by child sexual abuse.

http://www.isurvive.org/index.php

National support designed specifically for African-American men and women who were abused as children. Black Sexual Abuse Survivors: http://blacksurvivors.org/home

Partners of Adults Sexually Abused as Children http://www.pasac.net/

Peer support for partners of adults sexually abused as children.

Support for Partners http://www.supportforpartners.org

Books for Professionals and Parents of Children with Sexual Behavior Problems

The Stop Child Molestation Book: What Ordinary People Can Do In Their Everyday Lives To Save Three Million Children by Gene G. Abel, M.D. and Nora Harlow (Xlibris, December 2001) Order through amazon.com

Child Survivors and Perpetrators of Sexual Abuse: Treatment Innovations by Mic Hunter (Sage Publications, 1995)

Helping Children With Sexual Behavior Problems: A Guidebook for Professionals and Caregivers
by Toni Cavanagh Johnson, Ph.D. (3rd Edition, 2007)
Order this 44-page booklet from www.tcavjohn.com

The Relapse Prevention Workbook for Youth in Treatment
by Charlene Steen (Safer Society Press, 1999)

Report of the Task Force on Children with Sexual Behavior Problems
(Association for the Treatment of Sexual Abusers, 2006)
http://www.atsa.com/atsa-csb-task-force-report

The Sexualized Child in Foster Care: A Guide for Foster Parents and Other Professionals
by Sally G. Hoyle (CWLA Press, 2000)

Sexualized Children: Assessment and Treatment of Sexualized Children and Children Who Molest
by Eliana Gil and Toni Cavanaugh Johnson, Ph.D. (Self Esteem Shop II, 1992)

Sexually Aggressive Children: Coming To Understand Them
by Sharon K. Araji (editor) (Sage Publications, 1997)

Treating Children With Sexually Abusive Behavior Problems: Guidelines for Child and Parent Intervention
by Jan Ellen Burton (Haworth Press, 1998)

Treating Youth Who Sexually Abuse: An Integrated Multi-Component Approach
by Paul Steven Lundrigan (Haworth Press, 2001)

Understanding Children's Sexual Behaviors: What's Natural and Healthy
by Toni Cavanagh Johnson, Ph.D. (2003)
(This 20-page booklet is for parents, teachers, school counselors, social workers, police, and others who want to understand children's sexual behaviors.)
Order this and other helpful materials on assessment, investigations, interventions, and treatment through www.tcavjohn.com

Books to Educate Children About Preventing Sexual Abuse

It's My Body
by Lory Freeman (Parenting Press, 1984)

Keeping Kids Safe: A Child Sexual Abuse Prevention Manual
by Pnina Tobin, Sue Levinson Kessner (Hunter House Publishers; 2nd edition, 2002)

The Most Important Rule of All
by Pam Church
(Prevention And Motivation Programs, Inc., 1997) This book is a read-aloud storybook about child sexual abuse and protection skills for use with children ages 4-8 years.

My Body is Private
by Sandy Kleven (Illumination Arts Publishing, 1998)

Telling Isn't Tattling
by Kathryn Hammerseng (Parenting Press, 1996)

Those are MY Private Parts
by Diane Hansen (Empowerment Productions, 2005)
Parents and care-givers can use this read-aloud rhyme as a tool to teach children sexual abuse prevention and empower their young children to say NO. Appropriate for ages 4-8.

Your Body Belongs To You
by Cornelia Spelman (Albert Whitman & Co., 2000)

When I Was Little Like You
by Jane Porett (CWLA Press, 2000)

Resources to Educate Adults About Preventing Child Sexual Abuse

A Safer Family. A Safer World.
This booklet is designed for parents and caregivers of children 0-12 and is useful for childcare providers as well. The content is based on research and best practices of primary prevention, and attempts to focus on the proactive things that people can do and say, giving specific examples. The booklet is written at a 6th grade reading level, and is available in 10 languages.
http://depts.washington.edu/hcsats/csabooklet.html

5 Steps to Protecting Our Children
By Darkness to Light. Preventing, Recognizing, and Reacting Responsibly to Child Sexual Abuse - A Guide for Responsible Adults
www.d2l.org/

Do Children Sexually Abuse Other Children?
By Stop It Now!
http://www.stopitnow.org/downloads/Do_Children_Abuse.pdf

Hear Their Cries: Religious Responses to Child Abuse
This award-winning video on the role of clergy and lay leaders in
ending child abuse is a critical resource.
Order through FaithTrust Institute

Information for Parents on Child Sexual Abuse
by Speak Up Be Safe®
speakupbesafe.org/parents.html

*Preventing Sexual Abuse: Activities and Strategies for Those Working
With Children and Adolescents*
by Carol A. Plummer (Learning publications, 1997)

Stewards of Children Online Prevention Training
by Darkness to Light
http://www.d2l.org

Recovery and Support for Adult Survivors and Their Families

Allies in Healing: When the Person You Love Was Sexually Abused as a Child
by Laura Davis (Harper Paperbacks, 1991)

Beginning to Heal: A First Book for Survivors of Child Sexual Abuse
by Ellen Bass and Laura Davis (Perennial, 1993)

Beginning to Heal (Revised Edition): A First Book for Men and Women Who Were Sexually Abused As Children
by Ellen Bass, Laura Davis (Collins, 2003)

Betrayal of Innocence: Incest and its Devastation
by Susan Forward and Craig Buck (Penguin Books, 1998)

Beyond Betrayal: Taking Charge of Your Life after Boyhood Sexual Abuse
by Richard B. Gartner, William Pollack (John Wiley & Sons, 2005)

Beyond The Tears: A True Survivor's Story
by Lynn C. Tolson (Authorhouse, 2003)

The Courage to Heal: A Guide for Women Survivors of Child Sexual Abuse
by Ellen Bass and Laura Davis (Harpers Perennial, 3rd revised edition, 1994)

The Courage to Heal Workbook: A Guide for Women Survivors of Child Sexual Abuse
by Laura Davis (Perennial Currents, 1990)

Families in Recovery: Working Together to Heal the Damage of Childhood Sexual Abuse
by Beverly Engel, MFT (McGraw Hill Contemporary Books, March 2000)

From Victim to Survivor: Women Survivors of Female Perpetrators
by Juliann Mitchell, Juliann Whetsell-Mitchell and Jill Morse (Taylor & Francis, Inc., September 1997)

Ghosts in the Bedroom: A Guide for the Partners of Incest Survivors
by Ken Graber (Health Communications, 1991)

Healing Years: A Documentary about Surviving Incest and Child Sexual Abuse
Without recovery, survivors of child sexual abuse face emotional struggle, substance abuse, post-traumatic stress, and the perpetration of abuse in their lives and families. This artfully produced documentary illustrates the poignant stories of incest survivors: former Miss America, Marilyn Van Deburr speaking out in the nation, Janice Mirikitani, President of Glide memorial Church, San Francisco, helping inner-city women substance abusers healing from incest, and Barbara Hamilton, a 79-year old survivor ending three generations of incest in her family. For the sexually abused child, awareness and recovery is key to a secure and nourishing future. The Healing Years points the way.
Order through BIG VOICE PICTURES

I Never Told Anyone: Writings by Women Survivors of Child Sexual Abuse
by Ellen Bass (Perennial Currents, 1991)

I Will Survive: The African-American Guide to Healing from Sexual Assault and Abuse
by Lori S. Robinson (Avalon Publishing Group, 2003)

Misinformation Concerning Child Sexual Abuse and Adult Survivors
by Charles L. Whitfield, Joyanna L. Silberg, and Paul Jay Fink
(Haworth Press, July 2002)

Mothers Book: How to Survive the Molestation of Your Child
For and about mothers of survivors. This book answers the most common questions asked by mothers about their own emotional reactions, their relationship with the victim and the offender, their cultural and religious concerns and the criminal justice process.
Order through FaithTrust Institute

No Secrets, No Lies: How Black Families Can Heal From Sexual Abuse
by Robin D. Stone (Broadway Books, 2004)

The Obsidian Mirror: Healing from Childhood Sexual Abuse
by Louise M. Wisechild (Seal Press, 2003)

Secret Survivors: Uncovering Incest and Its Aftereffects in Women
by E. Sue Blume (Ballentine Books, 1991)

Resources for Divorce Care

Books from my Library

When the Vow Breaks by Joseph Warren Kniskern

What to do when you don't know what to do: Divorce and lost love God will Make a Way by Dr. Henry Cloud and Dr. John Townsend

Finding Hope After Divorce by Kay Arthur

Marriage, Divorce and Remarriage in the bible by Jay E Adam

Healing the Brokenhearted by Joyce Meyer

Moving forward in God's Grace: Celebrate Recovery the Journey continues by John and Johnny Baker

Hope for the Separated by Gary Chapman

Beyond the Broken Heart: A Journey through grief by Julie Yarbrough

Growing through Divorce by Jim Smoke

When you've been wronged: Moving from bitterness to forgiveness by Erwin W. Lutzer

Helping Children Survive Divorce by Dr. Archibald D. Hart

The children of Divorce: the loss of Family as the loss of being by Andrew Root

Christian Counseling Centers

Lifeline Christian Counseling Center
1979 E. Garfield Ave
Salt Lake City, UT 84108
801 455- 6006

El- Shaddai Counseling & Consulting Services
40 exchange place, TRS professional Suites 3rd floor
NY, NY 10005
917 804- 0931

Dr. Jean Paglia
Faith and Healing Ministries
326 Rutherford Avenue
Lyndhurst, New Jersey 07071
Faithandhealingministries.com
201 939-2515

Christian Wellness Center of NJ
225 DeMott Ln # 203
Somerset, NJ 08873
732 873- 2777
CWCNJ.org

Heart to Heart Counseling Center
1130 Route 202
South Building E Suite 5
Raritan, NJ
908 864 -0575
www.h2hcc.org

Wellsprings Counselling Center LLC
Fair Lawn, NJ
Hoboken, NJ
Montclair, NJ
Mountain lakes, NJ
New York City, NY
201 956 6363
Washingtonville, NY
845 496 - 6311
Wellsprings.org

Christian Counseling Center
391 S Dublin Pike,
Dublin PA, 18917
215 249 - 3232

BIBLIOGRAPHY

http://www.archive.acf.hss.gov/programs/cb/pups/cm10/cm.pdf

http://www.Victimsofcrime.org/Media/reporting-on-child-sexual-abuse/disclosures-statatics

http://www.childhelp.org/

http://www./darkness.2light.org/

Htttp://www.report.cybertip.org/index.htm

http://www.national childrensalliance.org

http://www.stopitnow.org./

http://www.justice for children.org

NSOPW.gov –raising awareness about sexual abuse Facts and Statistics.

UNIECF.org

Journal of Adolescent Health, Vol. 51, Issue 1, p-18-24

"Child Sexual Abuse: What Parents Should Know," American Psychological Association. (http://www.apa.org/pi/families/resources/child-sexual-abuse.aspx) (February 19, 2014)

Douglas, E., and D. Finkelhor, *Childhood Sexual Abuse Fact Sheet, Crimes Against Children* Research Center, May 2005. (http://www.unh.edu/ccrc/factsheet/pdf/CSA-FS20.pdf) (December 21, 2011)

Finkelhor, D., "The Prevention of Childhood Sexual Abuse," *Future of Children,* 2009, 19(2):169–94.

Kilpatrick, D., R. Acierno, B. Saunders, H. Resnick, C. Best, and P. Schnurr, *"National Survey of Adolescents,"* Charleston, SC: Medical University of South Carolina, National Crime Victims Research and Treatment Center, 1998.

"Sexual Assault of Young Children as Reported to Law Enforcement: Victim, Incident, and Offender Characteristics," U.S. Department of Justice, Bureau of Justice Statistics, 2000.

"National Crime Victimization Survey," U.S. Department of Justice, Bureau of Justice Statistics, 1996.

Silverman, J. G., A. Raj, L. A. Mucci, and J. E. Hathaway, "Dating Violence Against Adolescent Girls and Associated Substance Use, Unhealthy Weight Control, Sexual Risk Behavior, Pregnancy, and Suicidality," *Journal of the American Medical Association,* 2001, Vol. 286 (No. 5)

Printed in the United States
By Bookmasters